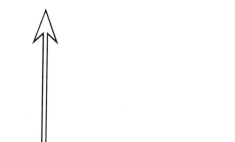

Xamarin.Forms
Kickstarter 2.0

Falko Schindler

Compilable Code Examples
for Solving Typical Cross-platform Tasks

Perpetual Mobile GmbH
Hohenholter Straße 43
48329 Havixbeck, Germany

www.perpetual-mobile.de

ISBN-10: 1523254629
ISBN-13: 978-1523254620

An online version of this book is available at www.xforms-kickstarter.com.

To gain access to the GitHub repository with the complete source code, send us an email with your GitHub user name and a selfie of you and this book: kickstarter@perpetual-mobile.de.

Contents

Foreword

It is a great pleasure to see this book published. As Joel Spolsky said: "Shipping is a feature. A really important feature. Your product must have it." We at Perpetual Mobile live this by heart. We create cross-platform apps for our customers and help them to get leaner and more agile while doing so.

When Falko first approached me with the idea to write a book about Xamarin.Forms, I could feel his enthusiasm and passion for it. He began developing apps around the same time Xamarin.Forms had its initial public release. Falko experienced first hand what it meant to be new to app development in general and Xamarin.Forms specifically. We immediately used the framework in customer projects, which has not always been easy and sometimes even frustrating. But after six months knee-deep in this young framework our team had built up a lot of knowledge. Inspired by Stack Overflow questions and answers Falko wrote in this time, he was eager to produce a set of *recipes* to supplement Xamarin's own documentation and existing books. A wonderful idea I was more than happy to support.

The book's compact, focused chapters make it a great resource for our day to day work with Xamarin.Forms. The exclamation "We have a chapter about that!" has become an idiom at our office. And whenever we wondered how to achieve something with Forms, the book grew by a new section. This never happened for Windows Phone. While it's a nice platform and general framework support would make it quite easy, the market share is much to low to spend any customer money on it. In our experience cross-platform mobile development means to make sure it runs on Android and iOS. Supporting both in a good fashion has never been easier than today. Thanks to Xamarin.Forms, developers now have a time and cost effective solution to build a good user interface with a platform specific user experience.

Creating such a powerful framework is a huge undertaking. The stretch between nativeness and *write once run everywhere* means a lot of effort for the guys at Xamarin. Right now you still need to write a lot of platform specific code if you care about true native looks, e.g. disclosure indicators on iOS, navigation drawer/flyout menu and material design. That's ok. No one can expect Xamarin to shoot silver bullets from a golden hammer. Xamarin.Forms is still in its scaffolding phase. Once the major bugs are rooted out and all basic concepts are settled, keeping up with the native platforms' newest innovations over the years will be the greatest challenge. But it can be used for production right now. And that is the important part. The major feature of Xamarin.Forms.

Do the same. Read this book. Build a nice app. And then ship it. It's the major feature, you know!

Rodja Trappe
CEO/CTO of Perpetual Mobile GmbH

Preface

When beginning to work at Perpetual Mobile[1], a startup company in Germany, dedicated to built high-quality mobile apps, I had zero knowledge about app development. Neither did I know about Xamarin, the development environment my team used for cross-platform projects with high percentages of shared code.

Within my very first weeks working in this new business, a new buzz word came up, which we couldn't ignore: Xamarin released Xamarin.Forms, a framework not only for sharing business code between iOS, Android and Windows Phone, but for sharing the UI description as well. Although my colleagues had developed a similar framework for one of our customers, we were vastly excited about trying Xamarin.Forms and using it for real-life projects.

It so happened, that I took my first steps in mobile app development with Xamarin.Forms, which proved to be perfectly suited in my situation: Despite my background in software development, I had to learn quite a lot regarding mobile devices, differences between Android and iOS, the deployment process and so forth. With Xamarin you not just "Write once, run everywhere" but also: "Learn once". Many tasks can be accomplished with shared code only, so you don't need to dive into the tedious details of each individual platform.

Of course, in some situations even Xamarin.Forms can get tough. I browsed the documentation, scoured the internet for demo code and asked on Stack Overflow[2] – my new favorite online platform. Whenever I found out how to implement a certain feature, I spent significant effort in simplifying the code, boiling it down to the bare minimum and improving the readability where possible.

Soon we came up with the idea to collect such code recipes and make them publicly available. So we launched the Xamarin.Forms Kickstarter website[3] in January 2015. The response was amazing. Even Miguel de Icaza, CTO and co-founder of Xamarin, expressed his support via Twitter.

After several code and text improvements, including additional chapters and addressing feedback from the Xamarin community, we decided to publish a printed version of this guide. For us, was a great chance to finalize the first 17 chapters and 36 example apps and focus on new exciting projects.

---

[1] http://www.perpetual-mobile.de/
[2] http://www.stackoverflow.com/
[3] http://www.xforms-kickstarter.com/

Remark on the second edition: the Xamarin.Forms Kickstarter 2.0

In November 2015, Xamarin released Xamarin.Forms 2.0 as part of Xamarin 4. Instead of introducing many new features, braking API changes and conceptual innovations, this major version rather stands for a new level of stability. In fact, Xamarin.Forms 2.0.0 *is* the stable 1.5.2 release with a "2.0" tag. After a year of improving the framework, fixing lots of bugs and tuning the performance, this release indicates a milestone.

Therefore, we decided to take the opportunity to release a corresponding edition of the Xamarin.Forms Kickstarter. We carefully revised all chapters, recompiled and tested all code examples against Xamarin.Forms 2.0, iOS 9.2 (unified API) and Android 6 (API level 23). And we added five new example apps and one whole new chapter about list views.

Luckily, most text and source code is still completely valid and didn't have to be modified. This is a pleasant indicator that this guide is rather stable and will probably remain applicable with future versions of Xamarin.Forms.

Source code access

For you, dear reader, it's not only an opportunity to purchase this updated guide for your desk, your team or the new co-worker not yet familiar with Xamarin.Forms. But you also get exclusive access to the GitHub repository containing 41 solutions with source code of all example apps shown in the book. Furthermore, you can follow the development of new examples and possibly another edition. As a proof of purchase, just send your GitHub user name and a selfie of you and this book to `kickstarter@ perpetual-mobile.de`.

About the code snippets

For each example app discussed in the book, all relevant source code is printed at full length. It is split into separate short snippets to add descriptive text closer to where it refers to. Instead of letting you alone with pages of class implementations, the book guides you through every required line of code.

All snippets have been automatically extracted from the original solutions using a BASH-driven process, so that typos and copy-paste mistakes are impossible. Every line of code is part of a compilable and tested code base and, thus, is guaranteed to work properly if correctly placed into an app project. Note that all examples are tested with the current Xamarin.Forms version 2.0.0.

While Xamarin supports Android, iOS and Windows Phone, this guide restricts to the first two platforms. Not only has Windows Phone a much lower market share, the two more common platforms suffice to demonstrate the cross-platform code-sharing in principle.

To save a significant amount of space, printed screenshots cover iOS versions only. Android behaves similarly – of course with its own native look. All apps are developed and tested for both iOS and Android.

Words of thanks

Let me address a few words of thanks to my colleagues for supporting this project where possible. It was our CEO and CTO Rodja Trappe, who got intrigued by the idea of writing a guide on Xamarin.Forms as quickly as I did and covered my back to let me keep focus on the Xamarin.Forms Kickstarter. Special thanks goes to Sascha Willam and Jan Oliver Zieger for lengthy code and text reviews. Furthermore, Sascha helped a lot to get the geolocation examples working and contributed significant parts of the corresponding source code. Last but not least, I'd like to thank Stephan Palmer and Maik Switalski for the many code reviews, pair-programming sessions and fruitful discussions, that are an integral part of the excellent working culture at Perpetual Mobile.

CHAPTER 1

Hello, Forms! – Our first cross-platform app

Our first app with Xamarin.Forms for iOS and Android is built in seconds.

In Xamarin Studio we create a new solution of type "Xamarin.Forms App" and choose an App name. For shared code we choose the "Use Shared Library" option. The new solution contains basically three projects: a shared project with all the cross-platform business logic and UI description as well as two projects with the platform specific integration and customization for Android and iOS devices.

In this chapter we will have a detailed look into each of these three projects.

The shared project

After creating a new Xamarin.Forms app, the shared project only contains one file named after your solution and defining the App class. It serves as the main entry point for the cross-platform code implementing both UI and business logic.

```
using Xamarin.Forms;

namespace HelloForms
{
    public class App : Application
    {
        public App()
        {
            MainPage = new ContentPage {
```

```
                    Content = new Label {
                        Text = "Hello, Forms!",
                        VerticalOptions = LayoutOptions.Center,
                        HorizontalOptions = LayoutOptions.Center,
                    },
                };
        }
    }
}
```

The constructor defines a new ContentPage filled with a Label. The Text is simply "Hello, Forms!". And the layout options just take care that it is nicely centered on the page.

This is all it takes to define the UI of our first cross-platform app. The following two sections will show how to integrate this shared project into platform-specific code.

The Android project

The Android project contains an activity named MainActivity. It is marked as MainLauncher and will appear on app start.

```
using Android.App;
using Android.Content.PM;
using Android.OS;
using Xamarin.Forms;
using Xamarin.Forms.Platform.Android;

namespace HelloForms.Droid
{
    [Activity(
        Label = "HelloForms.Droid",
        Icon = "@drawable/icon",
        MainLauncher = true,
        ConfigurationChanges = ConfigChanges.ScreenSize |
            ConfigChanges.Orientation)]
    public class MainActivity : FormsApplicationActivity
    {
        protected override void OnCreate(Bundle savedInstanceState)
        {
            base.OnCreate(savedInstanceState);

            Forms.Init(this, savedInstanceState);
```

```
            LoadApplication(new App());
        }
    }
}
```

After initializing Xamarin.Forms it loads a new instance of the platform-independent App.

Remark on the default namespace Droid

You might wonder why the default namespace of the Android project is named Droid and not Android – like it was the case in previous versions of Xamarin.Studio. If the namespace was Android, there could easily occur conflicts with the native Android namespace. Similarly, you should avoid creating solutions like "System", "Graphics" or "Forms" in order to avoid conflicts with very common namespaces.

The iOS project

The iOS project is similarly short: The method FinishedLaunching of the class AppDelegate initializes Xamarin.Forms and loads an instance of App.

```
using Foundation;
using UIKit;
using Xamarin.Forms;
using Xamarin.Forms.Platform.iOS;

namespace HelloForms.iOS
{
    [Register("AppDelegate")]
    public class AppDelegate : FormsApplicationDelegate
    {
        public override bool FinishedLaunching(UIApplication
            uiApplication, NSDictionary launchOptions)
        {
            Forms.Init();

            LoadApplication(new App());

            return base.FinishedLaunching(uiApplication, launchOptions);
        }
    }
}
```

Remark on the default namespace iOS

If you have source analysis enabled (Xamarin Studio Preferences → Text Editor → Source Analysis) you might get a warning that the namespace iOS should start with an uppercase letter. You can simply ignore it or change the name convention (Xamarin Studio → Preferences → Source Code → Name Conventions), since IOS would be a rather strange notation for "iOS" and it is nontrivial to rename the namespace together with all files and folders.

Figure 1.1: Our first Xamarin.Forms app. The page contains nothing but a horizontally and vertically centered label.

CHAPTER 2

Layouting – Positioning your content

In the previous chapter we created a simple page with one visual element only. If you want to layout multiple elements, Xamarin.Forms provides four possibilities:

○ A StackLayout aligns multiple child elements along one dimension, either horizontally or vertically.

○ A Grid allows for aligning visual elements in a grid-like structure.

○ A RelativeLayout provides constraints between position and/or size of its child elements.

○ An AbsoluteLayout allows you to specify absolute coordinates of each element.

First, we will create an example app containing all four layouting structures. Afterwards, we will demonstrate how to refer to the screen size for sizing and aligning visual elements and discuss Xamarin.Forms' layout options, two fundamental properties for controlling alignment and expansion of visual elements.

2.1   Comparison of Xamarin.Forms layouts

In the following example we will create a page with four content blocks, each built with one of these layouts. The visual appearance will be almost identical, but the implementation will be conceptually different.

The StackLayout – probably the most common layout in Xamarin.Forms – serves as the main layout containing the four blocks. With a platform-dependent padding the MainPage looks as follows:

17

```
MainPage = new ContentPage {
    Padding = new Thickness(0, Device.OS == TargetPlatform.iOS ? 20 : 0,
        0, 0),
    Content = new StackLayout {
        Children = {
            new DemoStackLayout(),
            new DemoGrid(),
            new DemoRelativeLayout(),
            new DemoAbsoluteLayout(),
        },
    },
};
```

The screenshot shows an overview of the final result. The "inbox" contains four item blocks, each with icon, name, subject, body and time. Before looking into each of the four layouts, we define classes for the single visual elements.

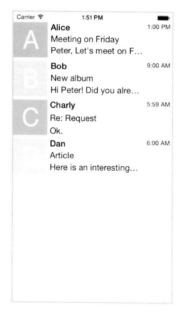

Figure 2.1: A dummy inbox showing four message previews, each of them implemented using a different layout structure: StackLayout, Grid, RelativeLayout and AbsoluteLayout (from top to bottom).

The Icon is a Label with large, white, centered text on a colored background. Text and color are passed to the constructor as arguments.

```
public class Icon: Label
{
    public Icon(string text, Color color)
```

```
    {
        Text = text;
        TextColor = Color.White;
        FontSize = 50;
        BackgroundColor = color;
        HorizontalTextAlignment = TextAlignment.Center;
        VerticalTextAlignment = TextAlignment.Center;
    }
}
```

The Name is a Label with bold text.

```
public class Name: Label
{
    public Name(string text)
    {
        Text = text;
        FontAttributes = FontAttributes.Bold;
    }
}
```

The Subject features a special truncation mode. Otherwise the possibly long string might not fit on the small mobile screen.

```
public class Subject: Label
{
    public Subject(string text)
    {
        Text = text;
        LineBreakMode = LineBreakMode.TailTruncation;
    }
}
```

The Body is actually identical to the Subject class. It is, however, reasonable to implement the extra class to allow for easy modifications later on, e.g. changing the text color of all subjects.

```
public class Body: Label
{
    public Body(string text)
    {
        Text = text;
        LineBreakMode = LineBreakMode.TailTruncation;
```

```
    }
}
```

And last but not least, the Time is a simple Label with rather small font size.

```
public class Time: Label
{
    public Time(string text)
    {
        Text = text;
        FontSize = 12;
    }
}
```

Note that Xamarin.Forms provides fields like HorizontalOptions and VerticalOptions as mentioned in the previous chapter. But here we restrict to specifying internal element properties only and leave the layout up to the wrapping layout classes.

Stack layout

The first block on our MainPage is a DemoStackLayout. It is derived from StackLayout, probably the most common layout in Xamarin.Forms. Since it allows stacking elements in one direction only, we need to combine multiple stacks hierarchically to obtain the desired result.

Like the main direction of one "email" block the DemoStackLayout is oriented horizontally. The Height-Request is 70 device-independent pixels, specifying the total height of the whole block. A Spacing of 5 pixels is almost identical to the default of 6 pixels.

Now we add three children: the Icon, another StackLayout and the Time label. We pass arguments like text and color to the constructors and set additional properties like the WidthRequest for Icon and Time.

```
public class DemoStackLayout: StackLayout
{
    public DemoStackLayout()
    {
        HeightRequest = 70;
        Spacing = 5;
        Orientation = StackOrientation.Horizontal;
        Children.Add(new Icon("A", Color.FromRgb(0.7, 0.8, 1.0)) {
            WidthRequest = 70,
        });
        Children.Add(new StackLayout {
```

```
            Spacing = 2,
            WidthRequest = 0,
            HorizontalOptions = LayoutOptions.FillAndExpand,
            Children = {
                new Name("Alice"),
                new Subject("Meeting on Friday"),
                new Body("Peter, Let's meet on Friday at 10 am"),
            },
        });
        Children.Add(new Time("1:00 PM") {
            WidthRequest = 50,
        });
    }
}
```

The nested StackLayout is oriented vertically (the default behavior) and has some tiny Spacing between its child elements. Zero WidthRequest and HorizontalOptions with expansion lets it occupy the available horizontal space – but not more. See Section 2.3 for a more detailed explanation of Xamarin.Forms LayoutOptions.

Note that the square shape of the icon is ensured by explicitly setting its WidthRequest to the same value like the blocks HeightRequest. Don't try to refer to the Width or Height properties of visual elements within the constructor. The element size will only be defined after adding the element to its parent and completing the (rather complex) Xamarin.Forms layout cycle.

Grid layout

In contrast to a StackLayout, the Grid allows for stacking content in two dimensions. And while a StackLayout is refined with nested layouts where needed, content of a fine-grained Grid can span multiple cells.

Our DemoGrid has the same HeightRequest and spacings like the DemoStackLayout. Before adding the five child elements, we only need to define rows and columns. This is done via a RowDefinitionCollection and a ColumnDefinitionCollection. A RowDefinition or ColumnDefinition can have a pre-defined Height or Width, respectively. Per default, the space is divided equally. We only specify the width of the first and last column, which is the Icon and the Time label. Note that the RowDefinitions with three equally sized rows is the default and can be neglected. The number of rows or columns would then be automatically derived from the children added afterwards.

Those child elements are identical to the ones added to the DemoStackLayout. Only the Add method is different: It allows specifying the grid cell coordinates (left, top) or even a range of cells (left, right, top, bottom). In our example only the Icon spans multiple cells, namely all three rows of the first column.

```
public class DemoGrid: Grid
```

```
{
    public DemoGrid()
    {
        HeightRequest = 70;
        RowSpacing = 2;
        ColumnSpacing = 5;
        RowDefinitions = new RowDefinitionCollection {
            new RowDefinition(),
            new RowDefinition(),
            new RowDefinition(),
        };
        ColumnDefinitions = new ColumnDefinitionCollection {
            new ColumnDefinition{ Width = new GridLength(70) },
            new ColumnDefinition(),
            new ColumnDefinition{ Width = new GridLength(50) },
        };
        Children.Add(new Icon("B", Color.FromRgb(0.8, 1.0, 0.8)), 0, 1, 0,
            3);
        Children.Add(new Name("Bob"), 1, 0);
        Children.Add(new Subject("New album"), 1, 1);
        Children.Add(new Body("Hi Peter! Did you already listened to the
            new album..."), 1, 2);
        Children.Add(new Time("9:00 AM"), 2, 0);
    }
}
```

Relative layout

After defining HeightRequest and both spacings as for the previous layouts, we make sure to set a non-expanding layout option using LayoutOptions.Start. Now it is reasonable to store all five elements into local variables, which we can refer to later. When adding them to the RelativeLayout, we can define functional constraints for their location and size. While we define width and height of the icon relatively to the parent layout l, the location of name, subject and body is defined relatively to other views v. So the name starts at the right edge of icon with some spacing and subject and body follow below. The time label is aligned to the right with a fixed width.

```
public class DemoRelativeLayout: RelativeLayout
{
    public DemoRelativeLayout()
    {
        HeightRequest = 70;
        const int xSpacing = 5;
        const int ySpacing = 2;
```

```
VerticalOptions = LayoutOptions.Start;
var icon = new Icon("C", Color.FromRgb(1.0, 0.8, 0.8));
var name = new Name("Charly");
var subject = new Subject("Re: Request");
var body = new Body("Ok.");
var time = new Time("5:59 AM");
Children.Add(icon,
    widthConstraint: Constraint.RelativeToParent(l =>
        l.Bounds.Height),
    heightConstraint: Constraint.RelativeToParent(l =>
        l.Bounds.Height));
Children.Add(name,
    xConstraint: Constraint.RelativeToView(icon, (l, v) =>
        v.Bounds.Right + xSpacing));
Children.Add(subject,
    xConstraint: Constraint.RelativeToView(name, (l, v) =>
        v.Bounds.Left),
    yConstraint: Constraint.RelativeToView(name, (l, v) =>
        v.Bounds.Bottom + ySpacing));
Children.Add(body,
    xConstraint: Constraint.RelativeToView(subject, (l, v) =>
        v.Bounds.Left),
    yConstraint: Constraint.RelativeToView(subject, (l, v) =>
        v.Bounds.Bottom + ySpacing));
Children.Add(time,
    xConstraint: Constraint.RelativeToParent(l => l.Bounds.Right -
        50),
    widthConstraint: Constraint.Constant(50));
    }
}
```

Absolute layout

The AbsoluteLayout is probably the most powerful layout. It allows you to specify absolute coordinates for all child elements. This might be an advantage for arbitrarily arranged elements, but can also be tedious if one of the previous layouts roughly matches the underlying structure.

Besides specifying the HeightRequest and horizontal spacing we pre-compute the width of the block with name, subject and body. To fill the available horizontal space completely, we need to refer to the screen width. In the next section we will describe in more detail, how to work with the screen size in the cross-platform code.

Now we add all five child elements, each with a Rectangle describing its layout bounds. The numbers represent left, top, width and height.

```
public class DemoAbsoluteLayout: AbsoluteLayout
{
    public DemoAbsoluteLayout()
    {
        HeightRequest = 70;
        const int xSpacing = 5;
        var centerWidth = App.ScreenWidth - 70 - 50 - 2 * xSpacing;
        Children.Add(new Icon("D", Color.FromRgb(0.8, 0.95, 0.95)), new
            Rectangle(0, 0, 70, 70));
        Children.Add(new Name("Dan"), new Rectangle(70 + xSpacing, 0,
            centerWidth, 23));
        Children.Add(new Subject("Article"), new Rectangle(70 + xSpacing,
            23, centerWidth, 23));
        Children.Add(new Body("Here is an interesting article."), new
            Rectangle(70 + xSpacing, 46, centerWidth, 23));
        Children.Add(new Time("6:00 AM"), new Rectangle(70 + centerWidth +
            2 * xSpacing, 0, 50, 70));
    }
}
```

While this implementation is very compact, it is nontrivial to read and to modify. Adding another element or changing some geometric property is difficult, since it would affect many lines of code. But whenever other layouts struggle to reproduce the desired content structure, an AbsoluteLayout is a reliable fallback solution.

2.2   Referring to the screen size

Xamarin.Forms' layout classes and options offer a powerful toolset for arranging visual elements on the mobile screen. In rare cases, however, you might want to compute positions or dimensions based on the current screen size. In the following example we want to create a set of colored squares that exactly fill the screen width, which is hardly doable without computing any lengths. Furthermore, defining the WidthRequest and HeightRequest is often significantly faster than leaving the layout negotiation to Xamarin.Forms.

A handy solution is to define a publicly accessible static ScreenSize property in some public class, e.g. App:

```
public static Size ScreenSize;
```

Since there is currently no platform-independent way to get the screen size, we initialize this property during FinishedLaunching on iOS:

```
App.ScreenSize = new Size(UIScreen.MainScreen.Bounds.Width,
    UIScreen.MainScreen.Bounds.Height);
```

and OnCreate on Android:

```
App.ScreenSize = new Size(
    Resources.DisplayMetrics.WidthPixels /
        Resources.DisplayMetrics.Density,
    Resources.DisplayMetrics.HeightPixels /
        Resources.DisplayMetrics.Density);
```

both right before calling the App constructor. Note that we need to consider the pixel density in order to get device-independent pixels.

The platform-independent App class will contain a grid of colored squares. Therefore, we define the page padding (the space between grid and screen boundary), grid spacing (the space between neighboring grid cells) as well as row and column count as constant class members:

```
const int padding = 10;
const int spacing = 5;
const int count = 5;
```

In the constructor, when the ScreenSize has been defined by the above-mentioned lines of code, we can compute the boxSize of a single square.[1] Furthermore, we create a new ContentPage filled with a custom ColorGrid. Padding and spacing are set as defined above.

```
public App()
{
    var boxSize = (ScreenSize.Width - 2 * padding + spacing) / count -
        spacing;

    MainPage = new ContentPage {
        Padding = padding,
        Content = new ColorGrid(boxSize, count, count) {
            RowSpacing = spacing,
            ColumnSpacing = spacing,
            VerticalOptions = LayoutOptions.CenterAndExpand,
        },
    };
```

---

[1]The box size b is computed as follows. The screen width w, padding p and spacing s are given in advance. So we can write $w = p + b + s + b + s + b + s + b + s + b + p$. Introducing the number of boxes $c = 5$ yields $w = 2p + c \cdot (b + s) - s$. We solve for b and obtain the box size $b = (w - 2p + s)/c - s$.

```
}
```

The ColorGrid is derived from the Xamarin.Forms layout Grid. The constructor takes three parameters: the size of each grid cell and the number of rows and columns. Two nested for loops add the requested number of cells. Each cell is a BoxView with pre-defined size and a color depending on its row and column indices.

```
public class ColorGrid: Grid
{
    public ColorGrid(double boxSize, int rows, int columns)
    {
        for (var row = 0; row < rows; row++)
            for (var column = 0; column < columns; column++) {
                var box = new BoxView {
                    Color = Color.FromRgb(row * 256 / rows, column * 256 /
                        columns, 127),
                    WidthRequest = boxSize,
                    HeightRequest = boxSize,
                };
                Children.Add(box, row, column);
            }
    }
}
```

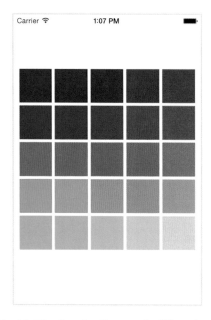

Figure 2.2: A Grid with 25 colored cells, exactly filling the width of the page.

2.3 What is the difference between Xamarin.Form's layout options?

In Xamarin.Forms every View has the two properties HorizontalOptions and VerticalOptions. Both are of type LayoutOptions and can have one of the following values:

- LayoutOptions.Start
- LayoutOptions.Center
- LayoutOptions.End
- LayoutOptions.Fill
- LayoutOptions.StartAndExpand
- LayoutOptions.CenterAndExpand
- LayoutOptions.EndAndExpand
- LayoutOptions.FillAndExpand

Apparently it controls the view's alignment on the parent view. But how exactly is the behavior of each individual option? And what is the difference between Fill and the suffix Expand?

Theory

The structure LayoutOptions controls two distinct behaviors:

1. **Alignment:**

   How is the view aligned within the parent view?

   - Start:
     For vertical alignment the view is moved to the top. For horizontal alignment this is usually the left-hand side. But note, that on devices with right-to-left language setting this is the other way around, i.e. right aligned.
   - Center:
     The view is centered.
   - End:
     Usually the view is bottom or right aligned. On right-to-left languages, of course, it is left aligned.
   - Fill:
     This alignment is slightly different. The view will stretch across the full size of the parent view. If the parent, however, is not larger then its children, you won't notice any difference between those alignments. Alignment only matters for parent views with additional space available.

2. **Expansion:**

   Will the element occupy more space if available?

○ Suffix Expand:

If the parent view is larger than the combined size of all its children, i.e. additional space is available, then the space is proportioned amongst child views with that suffix. Those children will "occupy" their space, but do not necessarily "fill" it. We'll have a look on this behavior in the example below.

○ No suffix:

The children without the Expand suffix won't get additional space, even if more space is available. Again, if the parent view is not larger than its children, the expansion suffix does not make any difference as well.

Example

To demonstrate the effect of different LayoutOptions, we create a tiny example app. It consists of a gray StackLayout with some padding and some spacing between its child elements.

```
static readonly StackLayout stackLayout = new StackLayout {
    BackgroundColor = Color.Gray,
    Padding = 2,
    Spacing = 2,
};
```

The constructor of our App adds eight child elements before assigning the StackLayout to the MainPage. Note that we use a device-dependent padding for the MainPage to avoid elements being overlaid by the iOS status bar.

```
public App()
{
    AddElement("Start", LayoutOptions.Start);
    AddElement("Center", LayoutOptions.Center);
    AddElement("End", LayoutOptions.End);
    AddElement("Fill", LayoutOptions.Fill);
    AddElement("StartAndExpand", LayoutOptions.StartAndExpand);
    AddElement("CenterAndExpand", LayoutOptions.CenterAndExpand);
    AddElement("EndAndExpand", LayoutOptions.EndAndExpand);
    AddElement("FillAndExpand", LayoutOptions.FillAndExpand);

    MainPage = new ContentPage {
        Padding = new Thickness(0, Device.OnPlatform<int>(20, 0, 0), 0, 0),
        Content = stackLayout,
    };
}
```

The method AddElement creates a new Label with different text and corresponding layoutOption. Its text is centered horizontally and vertically using the two properties HorizontalTextAlignment and VerticalTextAlignment.

Furthermore, it adds a flat yellow BoxView. This will serve as a visual separator between the space occupied by the white labels.

```
static void AddElement(string text, LayoutOptions layoutOption)
{
    stackLayout.Children.Add(new Label {
        Text = text,
        BackgroundColor = Color.White,
        HorizontalTextAlignment = TextAlignment.Center,
        VerticalTextAlignment = TextAlignment.Center,
        HorizontalOptions = layoutOption,
        VerticalOptions = layoutOption,
        WidthRequest = 160,
        HeightRequest = 25,
    });
    stackLayout.Children.Add(new BoxView {
        HeightRequest = 1,
        Color = Color.Yellow,
    });
}
```

The screenshot shows the resulting layout. We make the following observations:

○ The different alignment is only visible if there is space available. If the stackLayout would not fill the page, we might not be able to see a difference between elements with options Start or StartAndExpand.

○ Additional space is evenly proportioned amongst all labels with Expand suffix. To see this more clearly we added yellow horizontal lines – actually flat BoxViews – between every two neighboring labels. Labels with more space than their requested height do not necessarily "fill" it. In this case the actual behavior is controlled by their alignment. E.g. they are either aligned on top, center or label of their space or fill it completely.

○ If there is space available and no other expanding element – like in the horizontal direction – the alignment controls the element's position even if it is not expanding, like the first four labels.

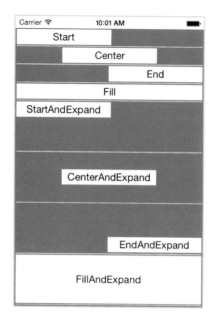

Figure 2.3: A `StackLayout` containing eight labels, each of them with different `HorizontalOptions` and `VerticalOptions`.

2.4   Brief introduction to XAML

So far – and for the remaining chapters – we implemented layout descriptions using C# code. There is, however, the possibility to use an XML-based layout description, namely the Extensible Application Markup Language (XAML).

The most obvious advantage is the imposed separation of layout and business logic. Furthermore, the XAML code *might* be shorter and more readable.

On the other hand, there are some drawbacks. Although XAML code can describe certain user interactions via bindings, more complicated interaction needs to be implemented within a so-called "code-behind" C# file. Thus, the layout description spreads across two files and two languages, which increases the complexity of our project structure. And since most of the XAML is only parsed at run-time, the code-completion, syntax-highlighting and source code analysis is incomplete and sometimes misleading.

Note that this is a rather personal opinion and the recommendation for XAML or C# might change with future Xamarin.Forms and Xamarin.Studio releases. Since nearly all features of Xamarin.Forms *can* be implemented using C# only, we restrict ourselves to C# within this book. But we don't want to withheld at least one XAML example.

In the following, we want to give a tiny example on how to create an app using Xamarin and an XAML layout description. Given a blank Xamarin.Forms solution, we add a new "Forms ContentPage Xaml" named "LabelPage" to the shared project. This generates two files: "LabelPage.xaml" with the XAML code as well as a nested "LabelPage.xaml.cs" with corresponding C# code.

First, let's look into the XAML part. The actual page content is framed by a ContentPage tag. It contains two URLs serving as scheme version definitions and the class definition LabelPage. Within this page we place a centered StackLayout with one Label and one Button. Besides corresponding Text attributes we assign names. This will allow us to refer to these two elements from C# code.

```xml
<?xml version="1.0" encoding="UTF-8"?>
<ContentPage xmlns="http://xamarin.com/schemas/2014/forms"
    xmlns:x="http://schemas.microsoft.com/winfx/2009/xaml"
    x:Class="Xaml.LabelPage">
    <StackLayout HorizontalOptions="CenterAndExpand"
        VerticalOptions="CenterAndExpand">
        <Label x:Name="helloLabel" Text="Hello, XAML!" />
        <Button x:Name="clickButton" Text="Click me!" />
    </StackLayout>
</ContentPage>
```

The corresponding C# file contains a partial class definition for our custom LabelPage. The constructor calls a method InitializeComponent, which is implemented in a different part of the class definition.

```csharp
public partial class LabelPage : ContentPage
{
    public LabelPage()
    {
        InitializeComponent();
    }
}
```

During compile time, Xamarin will parse the XAML file and create another C# file "LabelPage.xaml.g.cs" ("g" for *generated*) located in the "obj" folder. It contains the implementation of InitializeComponent, which in turn calls LoadFromXaml, the XAML parser.

The MainPage is now initialized with a new LabelPage.

```csharp
MainPage = new LabelPage();
```

To implement a simple user interaction, we access the two UI elements by name:

```csharp
var label = MainPage.FindByName<Label>("helloLabel");
var button = MainPage.FindByName<Button>("clickButton");
```

Then we can implement a button click handler as usual:

```
button.Clicked += (sender, e) => label.Text = "You did it!";
```

Note that we could also move the click handler implementation to the "LabelPage.xaml.cs" file. During InitializeComponent the generated C# code will store two private member variables helloLabel and clickButton. It allows us to assign the delegate (sender, e) => helloLabel.Text = "..."; to the event clickButton.Clicked anywhere within the LabelPage class after InitializeComponent has been called. This way we encapsulate both layout and user interaction in one class.

Figure 2.4: A XAML-based screen layout. After clicking the button (left), we see a different label text (right).

CHAPTER 3

Custom views – Beyond Xamarin's default elements

On of the most powerful features of Xamarin.Forms is its capability of working with natively implemented extensions of its default elements. If we wish to modify a visual element in some way or add new properties, we can derive a custom renderer with a platform-specific implementation. This can involve a custom visualization or even custom gesture-based user interaction.

3.1 A custom label renderer

In this example we will extend the Label element by a border color, border width and a corner radius for rounded corners. After discussing the platform-independent code of this CustomLabel, we will look into the corresponding iOS and Android renderer.

The platform-independent shared code

As mentioned above, the CustomLabel is derived from Label with three new properties: a border color, a border width and a corner radius:

```
public class CustomLabel: Label
{
    public Color BorderColor { get; set; }

    public double BorderWidth { get; set; }
```

```
    public double CornerRadius { get; set; }
}
```

Within the constructor of the App class we place a new CustomLabel on the MainPage. Besides the default properties like Text and BackgroundColor we can assign our new properties as well.

```
MainPage = new ContentPage {
    Content = new CustomLabel {
        Text = "A custom label",
        BackgroundColor = Color.Red.WithLuminosity(0.8),
        BorderColor = Color.Red,
        BorderWidth = 5,
        CornerRadius = 10,
        HorizontalOptions = LayoutOptions.CenterAndExpand,
        VerticalOptions = LayoutOptions.CenterAndExpand,
        WidthRequest = 200,
        HeightRequest = 50,
        HorizontalTextAlignment = TextAlignment.Center,
        VerticalTextAlignment = TextAlignment.Center,
    },
};
```

The layout options, size requests and alignments are just for centering the label on the page, enforcing a certain element size and centering the label text within the element bounds.

So far, the CustomLabel is derived from Label and will be displayed as such, i.e. with neither rounded corners nor a visible border. But in the next step we will override the corresponding iOS and Android renderers with a custom implementation considering all newly introduced properties.

The iOS renderer

A custom renderer needs to be implemented in the platform-specific project. Therefore, we add a new class CustomLabelRenderer to the iOS project.

The first thing we need to tell the compiler is that this will be the renderer associated with our CustomLabel:

```
[assembly:ExportRenderer(typeof(CustomLabel), typeof(CustomLabelRenderer))]
```

Sometimes a custom renderer only redefines some properties within the constructor. But in this case, we override the Draw method. Within the current drawing context we clear the canvas and then draw a rounded rectangle. These two methods are defined below.

```
public override void Draw(CGRect rect)
{
    using (var context = UIGraphics.GetCurrentContext()) {
        ClearCanvas(context, rect);
        FillRoundedRect(context, rect);
    }
}
```

On iOS it is required to clear the canvas by filling the rectangular area with white color. Otherwise we would see a black background.

```
static void ClearCanvas(CGContext context, CGRect rect)
{
    context.SetFillColor(Color.White.ToCGColor());
    context.FillRect(rect);
}
```

Drawing with "Core Graphics" – as indicated by the letters CG at some class names – usually works as follows: First we need to assign several properties like color, line width or stroke color of the current context. Then we add a new path representing the shape we want to draw. And finally we call DrawPath to actually draw the shape to the canvas.

Note that we need to convert the Xamarin.Forms color White using the method ToCGColor before using it within the Core Graphics context.

The very same pattern is used to draw a filled rounded rectangle. To access properties of our CustomLabel, we can use the Element member. Since the CustomLabelRenderer is derived from LabelRenderer, Element is already of type Label and can be cast to CustomLabel to get access to custom properties like Corner-Radius or BorderWidth.

```
void FillRoundedRect(CGContext context, CGRect rect)
{
    var label = Element as CustomLabel;
    var radius = (float)label.CornerRadius;
    var width = (float)label.BorderWidth;
    context.SetLineWidth(width);
    context.SetStrokeColor(label.BorderColor.ToCGColor());
    context.SetFillColor(label.BackgroundColor.ToCGColor());
    context.AddPath(CGPath.FromRoundedRect(rect.Inset(width, width),
        radius, radius));
```

```
        context.DrawPath(CGPathDrawingMode.FillStroke);
}
```

Note the method Inset: It creates a rectangle that is width pixels smaller then rect. Insetting the original rectangle is necessary in order to completely see the wide border on the canvas.

The Android renderer

In principle, implementing custom renderers on Android is very similar to iOS. The native drawing library, however, is slightly different.

To connect our CustomLabel with the CustomLabelRenderer for Android, the assembly attribute is identical to iOS. So we add a new class to the Android project and paste the following line:

```
[assembly:ExportRenderer(typeof(CustomLabel), typeof(CustomLabelRenderer))]
```

In contrast to iOS, we need to tell the Android renderer to actually call its Draw method by disabling SetWillNotDraw:

```
public CustomLabelRenderer()
{
    SetWillNotDraw(false);
}
```

Now we can override the Android Draw method. The Android renderer has an Element field as well, which allows us to access the visual element we need to draw. Here, we get a Canvas object, which works similar to the context on iOS. For example, it has a ClipBounds property describing the accessible drawing area. We will draw the label in three steps: First we fill the rectangle, then we draw the border, and finally we draw the label text.

```
public override void Draw(Canvas canvas)
{
    var label = Element as CustomLabel;
    var width = (int)label.BorderWidth * Resources.DisplayMetrics.Density;
    var radius = (float)label.CornerRadius *
        Resources.DisplayMetrics.Density;

    var rect = new RectF(canvas.ClipBounds);
    rect.Inset(width, width);

    FillRect(canvas, rect, radius);
```

```
    DrawStroke(canvas, rect, radius, width);
    DrawText(canvas, rect, label.Text);
}
```

On Android we usually work with a `Paint` object. It contains information like color, stroke with or whether we want to use anti-aliasing. The latter is a technique to avoid "staircases" when drawing sloped lines and shapes, which generally yields more visually pleasing results at the cost of slightly more computing time. The paint is then passed to the actual drawing method.

```
void FillRect(Canvas canvas, RectF rect, float radius)
{
    var paint = new Paint {
        Color = Element.BackgroundColor.ToAndroid(),
        AntiAlias = true,
    };
    canvas.DrawRoundRect(rect, radius, radius, paint);
}
```

Drawing a stroke works almost identically. We only need to define a `StrokeWidth` and set the paint style to `Stroke`. Note that in contrast to accessing the `BackgroundColor`, which is defined for every `Label`, we need to cast the `Element` to our `CustomLabel` in order to access the new property `BorderColor`. Furthermore, we need to convert the Xamarin.Forms color to an Android color using the method `ToAndroid`.

```
void DrawStroke(Canvas canvas, RectF rect, float radius, float width)
{
    var paint = new Paint {
        Color = (Element as CustomLabel).BorderColor.ToAndroid(),
        StrokeWidth = width,
        AntiAlias = true,
    };
    paint.SetStyle(Paint.Style.Stroke);
    canvas.DrawRoundRect(rect, radius, radius, paint);
}
```

The Paint class even has properties for drawing text. Thus, we can define the `TextSize` – using the display `Density` to convert from device-independent pixels to device-dependent pixels.

```
void DrawText(Canvas canvas, RectF rect, string text)
{
    var paint = new Paint {
        TextSize = (float)Element.FontSize *
            Resources.DisplayMetrics.Density,
```

```
    };
    var position = CenterText(paint, rect, text);
    canvas.DrawText(text, position.X, position.Y, paint);
}
```

Drawing text at the correct position can get rather tricky, especially centering it on a given rectangular area. We can control horizontal alignment via the TextAlign property of the Paint class. But there is no such property for vertical alignment. Therefore, we suggest the method CenterText: It measures the bounds of a text with a given paint and computes the top left corner position as an offset to the center of the given drawing rectangle rect.

```
static PointF CenterText(Paint paint, RectF rect, string text)
{
    var bounds = new Rect();
    paint.GetTextBounds(text, 0, text.Length, bounds);
    return new PointF(
        rect.CenterX() - bounds.Width() / 2,
        rect.CenterY() + bounds.Height() / 2);
}
```

Figure 3.1: A label with border and rounded corners. These properties are not natively supported by Xamarin.Forms, but can be implemented using custom renderers.

3.2 Gesture-based interaction

Custom renderers are not only useful for displaying UI elements in a different way than usual, but they can also connect the shared code with platform-specific gesture detection. In the following example we will create a new UI element showing a red ball that can be moved around the screen.

The platform-independent shared code

The Ball element expands across the whole MainPage. The ball is red and centered using the position (0.5, 0.5). (Since we will exchange coordinates between shared and platform-specific code, we would need to convert between device-independent and -dependent pixels. Therefore, it is often useful to work with floating point coordinates relative to the element size. Thus, (0, 0) is the top left corner, (1, 1) is the bottom right corner.)

```
MainPage = new ContentPage {
    Content = new Ball {
        HorizontalOptions = LayoutOptions.FillAndExpand,
        VerticalOptions = LayoutOptions.FillAndExpand,
        Position = new Point(0.5, 0.5),
        Color = Color.Red,
    },
};
```

The Ball class is derived from the Xamarin.Forms BoxView.

```
public class Ball: BoxView
```

The only additional public property is the ball Position.

```
public Point Position { get; set; }
```

Another Point stores the offset between ball and touching finger. It will be used for computing the new ball position depending on the current finger location.

```
Point offset;
```

The Ball class has two public methods for handling finger gestures. The first one, Down, is called when a new finger touches the screen and computes the offset from current ball and finger coordinates.

```
public void Down(double x, double y)
{
    offset = new Point(x - Position.X, y - Position.Y);
}
```

Whenever an already touching finger moves, the second method Pan is called. Given the new finger position and the previously stored offset, it computes the new ball Position. Afterwards, we trigger OnPropertyChanged. On the platform-specific side this will cause a redraw of the UI element.

```
public void Pan(double x, double y)
{
    Position = new Point(x - offset.X, y - offset.Y);
    OnPropertyChanged();
}
```

So far we have implemented the platform-independent part of our new UI element. Now we create new custom renderers for each platform. They define how to draw a Ball and call the gesture handling methods.

The iOS renderer

First we add a new class BallRenderer to the iOS project. It is a partial class and derives from Box-Renderer.

```
public partial class BallRenderer: BoxRenderer
```

The partial keyword allows to spread the class implementation across multiple source code files. In our example we split the rendering part and the gesture recognition.

To link the shared UI element Ball with its iOS renderer, we add the following assembly attribute above the namespace definition.

```
[assembly:ExportRenderer(typeof(Ball), typeof(BallRenderer))]
```

We override the OnElementChanged method and add a line to trigger the drawing method whenever an element property changed. This will be the case when a touching finger moves and the ball position changes. The background color White clears the canvas. The screen would be red otherwise, since Ball derives from BoxView with a Color property set to Red.

```
protected override void OnElementChanged(ElementChangedEventArgs<BoxView>
    e)
{
    base.OnElementChanged(e);
    Element.PropertyChanged += (s_, e_) => SetNeedsDisplay();
    BackgroundColor = UIColor.White;
}
```

Finally, we override the Draw method. Using the Width and Height of the associated UI ball we compute the iOS screen coordinates. (Remember that we defined Position to contain relative coordinates.) Then, within the current drawing context, we set the fill color, create a small rectangle around the ball position, add an elliptical path defined by that rectangle and draw the path with drawing mode Fill.

```
public override void Draw(CGRect rect)
{
    var ball = Element as Ball;
    var x = ball.Position.X * ball.Width;
    var y = ball.Position.Y * ball.Height;
    using (var context = UIGraphics.GetCurrentContext()) {
        context.SetFillColor(ball.Color.ToCGColor());
        var ballRect = new CGRect((float)x - 10, (float)y - 10, 20, 20);
        context.AddEllipseInRect(ballRect);
        context.DrawPath(CGPathDrawingMode.Fill);
    }
}
```

After implementing – and testing – the rendering part, we add another file named "BallGesture" to the iOS project. But instead of creating a new class, we continue the partial class BallRenderer. (Note that we don't need another assembly attribute nor specifying the inheritance.)

```
public partial class BallRenderer
```

The touch gestures are handled with two separate methods. First, we override TouchesBegan, basically converting the touch location to relative coordinates and calling the platform-independent method Down.

```
public override void TouchesBegan(NSSet touches, UIEvent evt)
{
    base.TouchesBegan(touches, evt);

    var touch = touches.AnyObject as UITouch;
    if (touch != null) {
        var location = touch.LocationInView(this);
```

```
        (Element as Ball).Down(location.X / Element.Width, location.Y /
            Element.Height);
    }
}
```

Furthermore, we override TouchesMoved. The implementation is almost identical, but calls Pan in this case.

```
public override void TouchesMoved(NSSet touches, UIEvent evt)
{
    base.TouchesMoved(touches, evt);

    var touch = touches.AnyObject as UITouch;
    if (touch != null) {
        var location = touch.LocationInView(this);
        (Element as Ball).Pan(location.X / Element.Width, location.Y /
            Element.Height);
    }
}
```

Note that iOS provides two more methods for handling touch events: TouchesEnded is called when the finger is raised from the screen and TouchesCancelled is called when it leaves the screen, e.g. via the edges of the touchable area. In this example, however, we restrict to the two above-mentioned methods.

The Android renderer

On Android the custom BallRenderer is conceptually equal to iOS, but differs in many details. As on iOS, we need a new partial class BallRenderer.

```
public sealed partial class BallRenderer: BoxRenderer
```

The sealed keyword prevents other classes from deriving from BallRenderer and fixes a compiler warning when adding the constructor code given below. But before implementing the renderer, we make sure to add the assembly attribute to link the renderer with the shared UI element Ball.

```
[assembly:ExportRenderer(typeof(Ball), typeof(BallRenderer))]
```

For a custom renderer on Android, we always need to decide whether we will draw the element. Therefore, we set:

```
public BallRenderer()
{
    SetWillNotDraw(false);
}
```

Again, we need to trigger the drawing procedure when the element changed. For this purpose, there is the Invalidate command on Android.

```
protected override void OnElementChanged(ElementChangedEventArgs<BoxView>
    e)
{
    base.OnElementChanged(e);
    Element.PropertyChanged += (s_, e_) => Invalidate();
}
```

To draw the ball, we convert the position from relative coordinates to screen coordinates, clear the screen by drawing a large black rectangle and draw a circle with the Element's Color. (Note that we don't compute the circle radius from a device-independent measure. Consequently, its size might differ between iOS and Android.)

```
public override void Draw(Canvas canvas)
{
    var ball = Element as Ball;
    var x = ball.Position.X * ball.Width;
    var y = ball.Position.Y * ball.Height;
    canvas.DrawRect(canvas.ClipBounds, new Paint{ Color =
        Android.Graphics.Color.Black });
    canvas.DrawCircle((float)x, (float)y, 20, new Paint { Color =
        ball.Color.ToAndroid() });
}
```

For handling touch events, we create a new file "BallGesture" within the Android project and continue the partial class BallRenderer. As in iOS, we don't need another assembly attribute, the inheritance nor the sealed keyword.

```
public partial class BallRenderer
```

In contrast to iOS, we can handle all touch events in one overridden method OnTouchEvent. Depending on the Action, Down or Move, we call the shared methods Down or Pan with the computed relative touch coordinates.

```
public override bool OnTouchEvent(MotionEvent e)
{
    var x = e.RawX / Element.Width;
    var y = e.RawY / Element.Height;
    if (e.Action == MotionEventActions.Down)
        (Element as Ball).Down(x, y);
    if (e.Action == MotionEventActions.Move)
        (Element as Ball).Pan(x, y);
    return true;
}
```

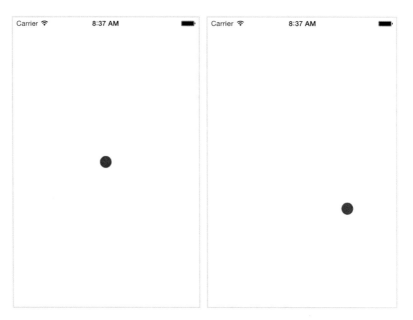

Figure 3.2: Screen with a red "ball" in its initial position (left) and after dragging it somewhere (right). The gesture-based interation is realized using custom renderers.

CHAPTER 4

Persistence – Don't forget a thing

In many situations we want to store values persistently, so that they are available when starting the app at some future time. Note that this can occur even if the user didn't kill the app in the meantime, but only moved it to the background. Usually the mobile operating system will decide on its own when to terminate an app and only keep a snapshot in the "recent apps" stack.

4.1   A persistent light switch using SimpleStorage

In this section we will focus on a solution based on the SimpleStorage NuGet package[1], which is our own development and allows you to store any serializable object from within shared code. We will implement an app with a light switch, which toggles the page's background color from white to gray and vice versa. Furthermore, it stores the current state persistently, so that the current state won't get lost when killing the app.

In order to use SimpleStorage, we need to add the corresponding package in both platform-specific projects. On Android you also need to add one line to `MainActivity.OnCreate` *before* `Forms.Init`:

```
SimpleStorage.SetContext(ApplicationContext);
```

Back in the shared project we can define a persistent property `IsLightOn` of our main class `App`.

---

[1]https://www.nuget.org/packages/SimpleStorage/

```
readonly SimpleStorage storage = SimpleStorage.EditGroup("light");

public bool IsLightOn {
    get { return storage.Get<bool>("on", true); }
    set { storage.Put<bool>("on", value); }
}
```

The commands for reading and writing values from the persistent storage consist of the following parts:

- EditGroup("light") defines the storage group. Small apps will usually need one group only. But for larger apps you might want to organize all the persistent variables into groups. It is recommended to store the storage group in a member variable like storage in this case to avoid duplicate code.

- Get and Put are methods to read and write persistent values. Asynchronous counterparts exist as well.

- <bool> is the data type of the persistent variable. This can be any serializable class.

- true is our default value for on in case there is no persistent variable with this name, yet.

To demonstrate the usage of such a persistent property we build a simple "light switch". First we define a label and a switch:

```
var label = new Label { Text = "Light?" };
var lightSwitch = new Switch();
```

Then we bind the IsToggled property of the latter to the App's IsLightOn property. Therefore we need to define the BindingContext, i.e. that object we're referring to, and the pair of properties we are binding, the IsToggledProperty and IsLightOn:

```
lightSwitch.BindingContext = this;
lightSwitch.SetBinding(Switch.IsToggledProperty, "IsLightOn");
```

The MainPage will contain a StackLayout with these two visual elements centered on the screen:

```
MainPage = new ContentPage {
    Content = new StackLayout {
        HorizontalOptions = LayoutOptions.CenterAndExpand,
        VerticalOptions = LayoutOptions.CenterAndExpand,
        Children = { label, lightSwitch },
    },
};
```

In order to see any visual feedback we define another binding between the page's BackgroundColor and the lightSwitch's IsToggled property:

```
MainPage.BindingContext = lightSwitch;
MainPage.SetBinding(VisualElement.BackgroundColorProperty, "IsToggled",
    converter: new ToggledToColorConverter());
```

Note that we need a value converter between the boolean IsToggled and the BackgroundColor of type Color. This can be done using a custom ToggledToColorConverter derived from IValueConverter:

```
class ToggledToColorConverter: IValueConverter
{
    public object Convert(object value, Type targetType, object parameter,
        CultureInfo culture)
    {
        return (bool)value ? Color.White : Color.Gray;
    }

    public object ConvertBack(object value, Type targetType, object
        parameter, CultureInfo culture)
    {
        throw new NotImplementedException();
    }
}
```

We only need to implement the forward conversion, which returns either Color.White or Color.Gray depending on the boolean parameter value.

4.2 Implicit persistence using a persistent bindable object

In the previous example, the persistence was managed withing the IsLightOn property. In case we need to implement many persistent values, it might be tedious to wire all of them with their storage. Therefore, we propose a *persistent* object class that reads and writes all its properties from and to storage automatically.

The implementation is surprisingly simple. But first, don't forget to set the SimpleStorage context within Android's MainActivity:

```
SimpleStorage.SetContext(ApplicationContext);
```

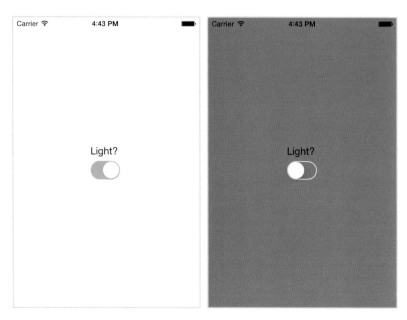

Figure 4.1: A persistent light switch. Its state, either on or off, is restored when starting the app. The background color is toggled accordingly.

The PersistentBindableObject derives from BindableObject for two reasons: It allows us to create bindings to visual elements. But most importantly, we'll make use of its built-in PropertyChanged event. The constructor has an optional key argument, which is used as edit group for SimpleStorage. If the key is null, we skip wiring the properties to SimpleStorage. (This might be handy if we need an instance of this class without persistence.) Finally, there are two important commands: First, we load each property from storage using the property name as key. Second, we subscribe to the PropertyChanged event to write the new value back to storage. That's all we need for our persistent bindable object.

```
public abstract class PersistentBindableObject: BindableObject
{
    protected PersistentBindableObject(string key = null)
    {
        if (key == null)
            return;

        foreach (var property in GetType().GetProperties())
            property.SetValue(this,
                SimpleStorage.EditGroup(key).Get<object>(property.Name));

        PropertyChanged += (sender, e) => {
            var property = GetType().GetProperty(e.PropertyName);
            SimpleStorage.EditGroup(key).Put<object>(e.PropertyName,
                (object)property.GetValue(this));
        };
```

```
        }
}
```

Let's make use of this new class. We'll implement a new class deriving from `PersistentBindableObject`.

```
public class Data: PersistentBindableObject
```

First, we need to implement the constructor with optional key. We simply call the base implementation with all the persistence magic.

```
public Data(string key = null) : base(key)
{
}
```

Now, we define bindable properties of different types. Even if we wouldn't want to use binding in our project, this mechanism is useful for automatically triggering the `PropertyChanged` event. Otherwise you'd need to call it manually within the properties' setters.

```
public static readonly BindableProperty StringProperty =
    BindableProperty.Create<Data, string>(p => p.String, "");
public static readonly BindableProperty NumberProperty =
    BindableProperty.Create<Data, double>(p => p.Number, 0);
public static readonly BindableProperty BooleanProperty =
    BindableProperty.Create<Data, bool>(p => p.Boolean, false);
```

Each `BindablProperty` get's its corresponding property of appropriate type. The getters and setters need to refer to their bindable property, such that Xamarin.Form's underlying implementation can react on changed properties and pass their values to bound objects.

```
public string String {
    get{ return (string)GetValue(StringProperty); }
    set{ SetValue(StringProperty, (string)value); }
}

public double Number {
    get{ return (double)GetValue(NumberProperty); }
    set{ SetValue(NumberProperty, (double)value); }
}

public bool Boolean {
    get{ return (bool)GetValue(BooleanProperty); }
```

```
    set{ SetValue(BooleanProperty, (bool)value); }
}
```

Now, before plugging everything into our MainPage, let's create a handy extension method to add binding to bindable objects. This method will work for all BindableObjects represented by the generic type T. First, it sets the BindingContext to the source object. Then it sets the actual binding between sourceProperty and targetProperty. Optional arguments of the SetBinding method (mode, converter and stringFormat) are made accessible just like in SetBinding.

```
public static class BindableObjectExtension
{
    public static T BindTo<T>(this T target, BindableObject source,
                              BindableProperty sourceProperty,
                              BindableProperty targetProperty,
                              BindingMode mode = BindingMode.Default,
                              IValueConverter converter = null,
                              string stringFormat = null)
        where T : BindableObject
    {
        target.BindingContext = source;
        target.SetBinding(targetProperty, sourceProperty.PropertyName,
            mode, converter, stringFormat);
        return target;
    }
}
```

Using our Data class and the handy BindableObjectExtension, we can create our MainPage in just a couple of lines of code. First, we instantiate an object of the Data class using the key "data". This will cause the PersistentBindableObject constructor to load all properties if they exist from a previous run.

```
var data = new Data("data");
```

The MainPage consists of six visual elements, all bound to different properties of the data object. The optional arguments like stringFormat allow to fine-tune the binding for individual elements.

```
MainPage = new ContentPage {
    Padding = new Thickness(10, Device.OS == TargetPlatform.iOS ? 30 : 10,
        10, 10),
    Content = new StackLayout {
        Children = {
            new Entry().BindTo(data, Data.StringProperty,
                Entry.TextProperty),
```

```
            new Label().BindTo(data, Data.StringProperty,
                Label.TextProperty),
            new Slider().BindTo(data, Data.NumberProperty,
                Slider.ValueProperty),
            new Label().BindTo(data, Data.NumberProperty,
                Label.TextProperty, stringFormat: "{0:0.00}"),
            new Switch().BindTo(data, Data.BooleanProperty,
                Switch.IsToggledProperty),
            new Label().BindTo(data, Data.BooleanProperty,
                Label.TextProperty),
        },
    },
};
```

Figure 4.2: Six visual elements bound to a persistent data object. Changing the entry text, moving the slider or toggling the switch causes immediate update of the corresponding labels. Furthermore, after restarting the app, all data is recovered.

Words of caution

Persisting *all* properties of an object is only recommended for pure data containers like our Data class and smaller projects where you can overlook all possible side effects. In more complex projects you might need a more advanced and explicit approach to persist your data. Classes that do a significant amount of business logic might cause problems just like inheritance with virtual and abstract properties.

Furthermore, the PersistentBindableObject persists its own derived property BindingContext. If you don't improve the implementation by excluding it explicitly, you should avoid setting data.Binding-Context. Otherwise you possibly send the given context object (maybe a visual element) to storage, which is usually not what you want. But in most cases the persistent bindable object will be the common binding context for many UI elements, so that data doesn't need a binding context.

4.3   Persisting single properties with a handy extension method

Can we simplify the use of SimpleStorage even further? Let's try to put all the magic of the afore-mentioned PersistentBindableObject into an extension method.

But first, don't forget to set the SimpleStorage context within Android's MainActivity:

```
SimpleStorage.SetContext(ApplicationContext);
```

The extension method Persist will have two arguments only (besides the bindable object obj itself): The property specifies which property to persist. And key defines the SimpleStorage edit group. The method will use the property name as storage key. The remainder is similar to the PersistentBindableObject implementation: The respective property is initialized with a value read from storage. And as soon as the property changes, it is written back to persistent storage. Since Persist returns the object itself, we can tightly attach the extension method to an object creation and even chain multiple calls.

```
public static class BindableObjectExtension
{
    public static T Persist<T>(this T obj, BindableProperty property,
        string key) where T: BindableObject
    {
        var storage = SimpleStorage.EditGroup(key);
        var propertyInfo = typeof(T).GetProperty(property.PropertyName);
        propertyInfo.SetValue(obj,
            storage.Get<object>(property.PropertyName));
        obj.PropertyChanged += (sender, e) => {
            if (property.PropertyName == e.PropertyName)
                storage.Put<object>(e.PropertyName,
                    (object)propertyInfo.GetValue(obj));
        };
        return obj;
    }
}
```

Our MainPage contains three visual elements, each with one persistent property. For both, creating the object and persisting one of its properties, we need one line of code only!

```
MainPage = new ContentPage {
    Content = new StackLayout {
        VerticalOptions = LayoutOptions.Center,
        Children = {
            new Entry().Persist(Entry.TextProperty, "entry"),
            new Slider().Persist(Slider.ValueProperty, "slider"),
            new Switch().Persist(Switch.IsToggledProperty, "switch"),
        },
    },
};
```

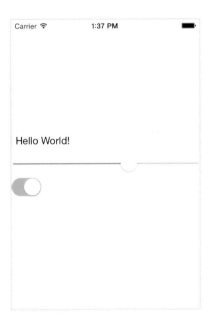

Figure 4.3: Three visual elements, each of them with one persistent property. Restarting the app will load their last values from persistent storage.

But be careful: Binding two properties to the same persistent storage will not cause one of them to get updated when the other one changes, since SimpleStorage does not observe the storage for changes. For inter-object binding you should use Xamarin.Forms' binding mechanism, possibly with a PersistentBindableObject as shown above.

CHAPTER 5

Navigation – More than flipping pages

So far we created single-page apps only. Usually, however, we want to navigate through multiple pages. After describing how to open and to close single pages, we will introduce a common pattern of list and detail pages. The latter is especially useful if there is a collection of similar objects, each with a correspoding page.

Note that "list and detail pages" are often referred to as "master and detail pages". Xamarin.Forms, however, uses a class called MasterDetailPage for a different concept, namely a slide-out menu (described in the last section of this chapter). Therefore, we will call a list with corresponding detail pages "list page".

5.1 Pushing and popping content pages

The following example demonstrates basic methods to navigate from one ContentPage to another.

The MainPage is initialized with a DemoPage, which we will define below, wrapped into a NavigationPage, which will create a navigation bar above the content.

```
public App()
{
    MainPage = new NavigationPage(new DemoPage());
}
```

On the DemoPage we put five buttons:

- ○ PushAsync:

  Open a new instance of DemoPage. The new page will be pushed onto the navigation stack.

- ○ PopAsync:

  Close the current instance of DemoPage. The page will be popped from the navigation stack.

- ○ PushModalAsync:

  Open a new instance of DemoPage presented *modally*. The modal page will slide in upwards.

- ○ PopModalAsync:

  Close the current modal page. The page will slide out downwards.

- ○ PopToRootAsync:

  Close all but the first instance of DemoPage. All other pages will be removed from the navigation stack.

Note the suffix Async: All five methods will run asynchronously.

```csharp
public class DemoPage: ContentPage
{
    public DemoPage()
    {
        Content = new StackLayout {
            Children = {
                new Button {
                    Text = "PushAsync",
                    Command = new Command(() => Navigation.PushAsync(new
                        DemoPage())),
                },
                new Button {
                    Text = "PopAsync",
                    Command = new Command(() => Navigation.PopAsync()),
                },
                new Button {
                    Text = "PushModalAsync",
                    Command = new Command(() =>
                        Navigation.PushModalAsync(new DemoPage())),
                },
                new Button {
                    Text = "PopModalAsync",
                    Command = new Command(() =>
                        Navigation.PopModalAsync()),
                },
```

```
                new Button {
                    Text = "PopToRootAsync",
                    Command = new Command(() =>
                        Navigation.PopToRootAsync()),
                },
            },
        };
    }
}
```

Figure 5.1: Five buttons, each triggering a different page transition.

5.2 Organize lists of detail pages

A common use case for content navigation is the following example. You have a list of objects that you want to present to the user. Furthermore, the user should be able to tap single list items to open a page with corresponding detailed information.

Again, the MainPage is just a NavigationPage containing a custom content page defined below.

```
public App()
{
    MainPage = new NavigationPage(new FruitListPage());
}
```

The content of the FruitListPage is a ListView. It has three important properties as well as an event handler for recognizing tap gestures:

- ItemsSource connects the ListView to a List which contains the items to be displayed. In this example it is a list of the custom class Fruit defined below.

- ItemTemplate defines how each item is displayed. Apposite to the Fruit items we will define a corresponding FruitCell.

- RowHeight is the height of each row. In order to encapsulate the complete layout definition into the FruitCell class, we define the RowHeight there and use it here.

- ItemTapped is the event of tapping a list item. The event handler is a delegate which deselects the currently selected item and pushes a new FruitDetailPage, which we will define below as well.

```
public class FruitListPage: ContentPage
{
    public FruitListPage()
    {
        var listView = new ListView {
            ItemsSource = new List<Fruit> {
                new Fruit { Name = "Apple", Description = "Awesome!" },
                new Fruit { Name = "Banana", Description = "Beautiful!" },
                new Fruit { Name = "Cherry", Description = "Cheap!" },
            },
            ItemTemplate = new DataTemplate(typeof(FruitCell)),
            RowHeight = FruitCell.RowHeight,
        };
        listView.ItemTapped += (sender, e) => {
            listView.SelectedItem = null;
            Navigation.PushAsync(new FruitDetailPage(e.Item as Fruit));
        };
        Title = "Fruits";
        Content = listView;
    }
}
```

The Fruit class only consists of two strings, a name and a description:

```
public class Fruit
{
    public string Name { get; set; }

    public string Description { get; set; }
}
```

The visual representation of a Fruit, the FruitCell, contains two labels arranged in a StackLayout. Their Text properties are bound to the corresponding Fruit properties. Note that we don't need to specify a binding context, since it is automatically set to the Fruit instance associated with the current cell.

```csharp
public class FruitCell: ViewCell
{
    public const int RowHeight = 55;

    public FruitCell()
    {
        var nameLabel = new Label { FontAttributes = FontAttributes.Bold };
        nameLabel.SetBinding(Label.TextProperty, "Name");

        var descriptionLabel = new Label { TextColor = Color.Gray };
        descriptionLabel.SetBinding(Label.TextProperty, "Description");

        View = new StackLayout {
            Spacing = 2,
            Padding = 5,
            Children = {
                nameLabel,
                descriptionLabel,
            },
        };
    }
}
```

Last but not least we define a page that is opened when tapping on a list item. Its Title is set to the Name of the current fruit. The Description is shown as a Label centered on the page.

```csharp
public class FruitDetailPage: ContentPage
{
    public FruitDetailPage(Fruit fruit)
    {
        Title = fruit.Name;
        Content = new Label {
            Text = fruit.Description,
            HorizontalOptions = LayoutOptions.CenterAndExpand,
            VerticalOptions = LayoutOptions.CenterAndExpand,
        };
    }
}
```

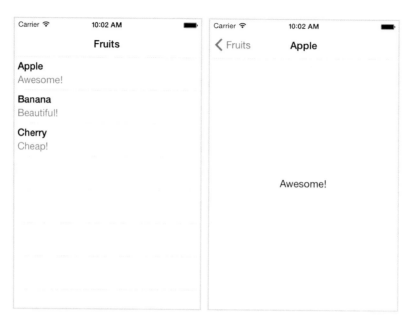

Figure 5.2: A list page (left) and one of the three detail pages (right).

5.3   A slide-out menu using a master-detail page

For structuring rather complex apps it is a common pattern to provide a slide-out menu. It is always accessible, even if the user navigates deep into the page hierarchy. So it allows to quickly switch between different parts of the app.

Xamarin.Forms provides a handy class for building such slide-out pages: We assign a new MasterDetail-Page to the MainPage. Its first part, the Master page, becomes our custom MenuPage. Secondly, the Detail page, is a new NavigationPage containing a LinkPage, which we'll define below. In order to be able to access this fundamental object, we assign it to a public static member variable.

```
public class App: Application
{
    public static MasterDetailPage MasterDetailPage;

    public App()
    {
        MasterDetailPage = new MasterDetailPage {
            Master = new MenuPage(),
            Detail = new NavigationPage(new LinkPage("A")),
        };
        MainPage = MasterDetailPage;
    }
}
```

The MenuPage contains three MainLinks, that will open page "A", "B" or "C". Note that – even if not displayed – the master page needs a page title, which is "Master" in our case. For better visibility use a grayish BackgroundColor. And if we want to see an icon in the top left corner indicating the "back-to-menu" button on iOS, we need to assign an Icon and add it to the iOS "Resources" folder. Otherwise we would see a link with the master page title "Master".

```
public class MenuPage: ContentPage
{
    public MenuPage()
    {
        Content = new StackLayout {
            Padding = new Thickness(0, Device.OnPlatform<int>(20, 0, 0),
                0, 0),
            Children = {
                new MainLink("Page A"),
                new MainLink("Page B"),
                new MainLink("Page C"),
            }
        };
        Title = "Master";
        BackgroundColor = Color.Gray.WithLuminosity(0.9);
        Icon = Device.OS == TargetPlatform.iOS ? "menu.png" : null;
    }
}
```

To open the menu the user can either tap the "Back-to-menu" button or swipe from left to right.

So how do we open a new page from the menu? The MainLink button simply assigns a new Navigation-Page to the Detail page. In order to hide the menu after tapping a MainLink, the IsPresented property is set to false.

```
public class MainLink: Button
{
    public MainLink(string name)
    {
        Text = name;
        Command = new Command(o => {
            App.MasterDetailPage.Detail = new NavigationPage(new
                LinkPage(name));
            App.MasterDetailPage.IsPresented = false;
        });
    }
}
```

The custom LinkPage shows three SubLink buttons. Each button is labeled with the name of the current page with an individual suffix.

```csharp
public class LinkPage: ContentPage
{
    public LinkPage(string name)
    {
        Title = name;
        Content = new StackLayout {
            Children = {
                new SubLink(name + ".1"),
                new SubLink(name + ".2"),
                new SubLink(name + ".3"),
            },
        };
    }
}
```

In contrast to a MainLink, the SubLink does not replace the detail page, but pushes a new LinkPage on the navigation stack.

```csharp
public class SubLink: Button
{
    public SubLink(string name)
    {
        Text = name;
        Command = new Command(o =>
            App.MasterDetailPage.Detail.Navigation.PushAsync(new
            LinkPage(name)));
    }
}
```

As soon as there is more than one LinkPage on the navigation stack, a "Back" button will appear in the top left corner allowing to close the current page.

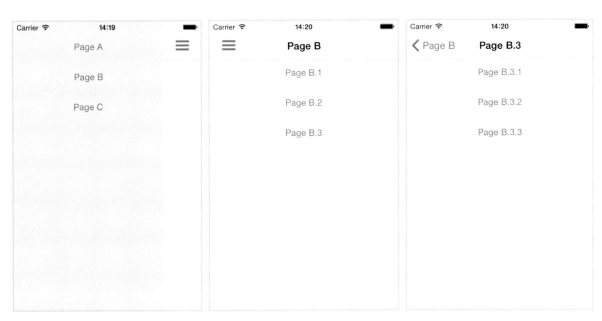

Figure 5.3: Demonstration of a MasterDetailPage navigation. The master page contains the main menu (left). Clicking a menu item closes the master page and shows a detail page (center). Pushing another page from a detail page opens a subpage (right).

CHAPTER 6

List view interaction – Add, delete and pull-to-refresh

Previously, we introduced list views as a way to organize a set of items with corresponding detail pages. In this chapter, we want to extend this handy element with additional functionality. With the current version of Xamarin.Forms you can easily implement things like swiping items to unveil additional context actions and the famous pull-to-refresh. To keep the examples short and clear, we will split these functionalities into separate apps described in separate sections.

6.1   Adding and removing items via context actions

In this example we display a list of grocery items. The user will be able to insert new items as well as to delete some of them. We'll implement the latter functionality using context actions, which were introduced with Xamarin.Forms 1.3.

Within the App constructor, we initialize an ObservableCollection filled with some strings.

```
var list = new ObservableCollection<string> { "Grapes", "Milk",
    "Potatoes", "Eggs", "Carrots" };
```

Note that we need to use an ObservableCollection instead of a List. Otherwise the ListView wouldn't be able to react on list manipulations like insertions or deletions.

The MainPage contains a new ListView bound to our list and with an ItemTemplate of type ItemCell, which we'll define in a minute. In order to be able to add toolbar items, the ContentPage is wrapped in a NavigationPage.

```
MainPage = new NavigationPage(new ContentPage {
    Title = "Shopping list",
    Content = new ListView {
        ItemsSource = list,
        ItemTemplate = new DataTemplate(typeof(ItemCell)),
    },
});
```

To allow the user to add new items, we add a ToolbarItem. When pressed, the MainPage will display an action sheet with three grocery items and a "Cancel" button. If the selected item is not the "Cancel" button, we'll add the item to the list. Since list is observable, the ListView will display the new item automatically.

```
MainPage.ToolbarItems.Add(new ToolbarItem {
    Text = "Add",
    Command = new Command(async o => {
        var item = await MainPage.DisplayActionSheet("Add item", "Cancel",
            null, "Butter", "Cream", "Onions");
        if (item != "Cancel")
            list.Add(item);
    }),
});
```

In order to allow the user to remove single items, we'll implement a Remove event within the ItemCell class. Here, in the App constructor, is a good place to subscribe to this event and implement the removal of the respective item.

```
ItemCell.Remove += item => list.Remove(item);
```

Note that subscribing to a static event without canceling the subscription later might cause a memory leak. In this artificial example, however, we'll ignore this issue.

Now we're only missing the ItemCell implementation. It basically derives from TextCell.

```
public class ItemCell: TextCell
```

The afore-mentioned event is defined as follows. It is public, static and requires a string argument identifying the item subject to deletion.

```
public static event Action<string> Remove = delegate { };
```

Note that the list could contain duplicate items. So the identity might be ambiguous. But in this simple example we'll ignore this issue.

Within its ItemCell constructor, we bind the cell's TextProperty to the item string itself. This is indicated by the path ".".

```
SetBinding(TextProperty, new Binding("."));
```

Furthermore, we create a new button with a caption "Remove". The IsDestructive property yields a red background color on iOS to indicate a destructive behavior. By binding the button's CommandParameter-Property to the item string, the string will be accessible when handling a Clicked event. Then we can invoke the static Remove event and pass the CommandParameter as an argument. Finally, we add the button to the cell's ContextActions.

```
var button = new MenuItem {
    Text = "Remove",
    IsDestructive = true,
};
button.SetBinding(MenuItem.CommandParameterProperty, ".");
button.Clicked += (sender, e) => Remove((sender as
    MenuItem).CommandParameter as string);
ContextActions.Add(button);
```

This list of context actions is unveiled by swiping a list item to the left on iOS and by long-pressing an item on Android. The whole interaction is shown in the screenshots below.

6.2 Pull-to-refresh

Another handy interaction scheme is the famous pull-to-refresh. It is built-in with Xamarin.Forms since version 1.4.

To demonstrate its behavior, we create a listView with an ItemsSource given by a custom method CreateList. We'll discuss its implementation shortly. To enable the pull-to-refresh interaction, we set IsPullToRefreshEnabled to true.

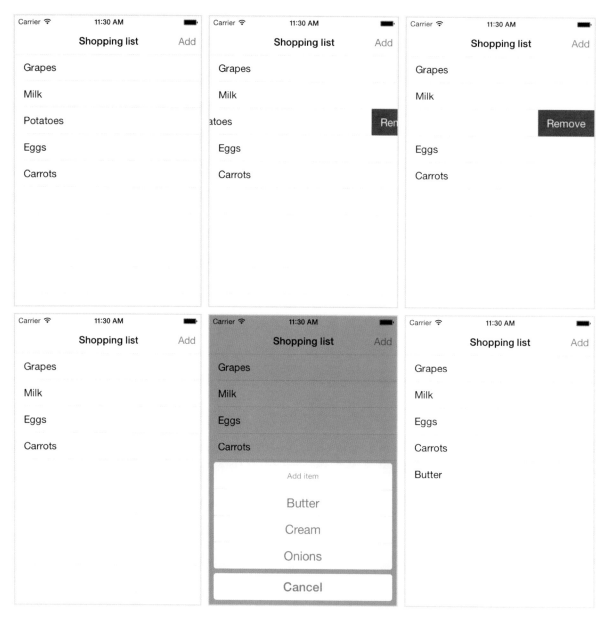

Figure 6.1: A shopping list with toolbar item and context actions. Swiping an item to the left unveils the context action "Remove". Pressing the "Add" button opens an action sheet allowing to insert a new item.

```
var listView = new ListView {
    ItemsSource = CreateList(),
    IsPullToRefreshEnabled = true,
};
```

Now we need to react, when the user pulled to refresh the list. Therefore, we subscribe to the list view's Refreshing event. First, we update the ItemsSource with another call to CreateList. Afterwards, we call EndRefresh to return to the normal, non-freshing state. The list view will move back to the top of the page and the spinning wheel will disappear.

```
listView.Refreshing += (sender, e) => {
    listView.ItemsSource = CreateList();
    listView.EndRefresh();
};
```

The MainPage contains nothing but the listView.

```
MainPage = new ContentPage {
    Padding = new Thickness(0, Device.OS == TargetPlatform.iOS ? 20 : 0,
        0, 0),
    Content = listView,
};
```

The CreateList method returns the current date and time in various formats. It selects each of 19 format specifiers and concatenates it with the current DateTime in the respective format. (Because we are calling DateTime.Now multiple times, their values – especially the milliseconds – might differ.)

```
static List<string> CreateList()
{
    var specifiers = new [] {
        "d", "D", "f", "F", "g", "G", "M", "m", "O", "o", "R", "r", "s",
            "t", "T", "u", "U", "y", "Y",
    };
    return specifiers.Select(format => format + ": " +
        DateTime.Now.ToString(format)).ToList();
}
```

The following screenshots show the outcome of this method as well as the update interaction via pull-to-refresh.

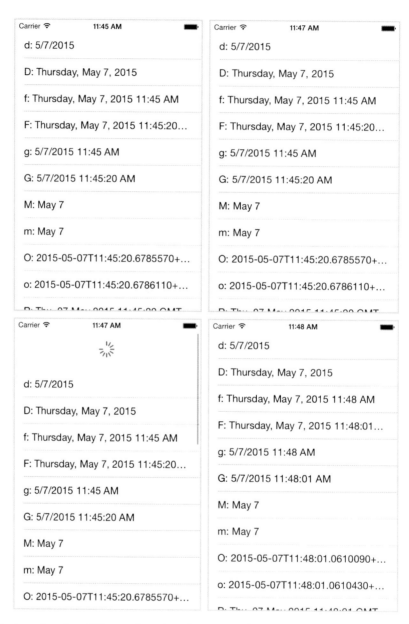

Figure 6.2: A list view showing different date-time formats. After a while, the list items are outdated and the displayed times are a few minutes behind (compared to the status bar in the second image). Pulling the list downwards unveiles a spinning wheel triggering a list update. Now the items match the system time.

Pictures – Spicing up your content

For some reason, you might want to add images to your app. It might be part of your app design, like a background image, or a set of small informative icons to underline the purpose of neighboring buttons or textual data.

7.1 Embedding images from different sources

Xamarin.Forms allows you to embed images from three different sources: local images (stored in the platform-specific file structure), embedded images (stored in the assembly as an embedded resource) and remote images (downloaded from the web).

Local images

To add a local image to the cross-platform app, you can simply drag the image file from your system's file manager into the Xamarin.Studio "Resources" folder on iOS and "Resources/drawable" folder on Android, respectively. The build action should be automatically set to "BundleResource" and "AndroidResource". Then you can create an Image as follows.

```
Content = new Image {
    Source = ImageSource.FromFile("xamarin.png"),
},
```

Embedded images

An embedded image can be stored in the shared project. Just make sure to set the build action to "EmbeddedResource" and assign a Resource ID, "xamarin" in this example. This ID is then used to refer to the image:

```
Content = new Image {
    Source = ImageSource.FromResource("xamarin"),
},
```

Remote images

Last but not least, we can refer to an online resource. Obviously, this method might cause some delay, which affects the user experience. Or even worse: They might be unavailable due to missing internet connection. Thus, we should download images only if they are unavailable at compile time.

```
Content = new Image {
    Source = ImageSource.FromUri(new Uri("http://tinyurl.com/nmd85s3"))
},
```

The resulting screen is identical for all image sources.

Figure 7.1: Page with one centered image. The screen is identical for local, embedded and remote images.

7.2 Comparison of possible aspect ratios

The most useful Image property is the Aspect ratio with three possible values. To demonstrate them side-by-side, we create a TabbedPage with one embedded image per ContentPage.

```
MainPage = new TabbedPage {
    Children = {
        new ContentPage {
            Title = "AspectFill",
            Content = new Image {
                Source = ImageSource.FromResource("xamarin"),
                Aspect = Aspect.AspectFill,
            },
        },
        new ContentPage {
            Title = "AspectFit",
            Content = new Image {
                Source = ImageSource.FromResource("xamarin"),
                Aspect = Aspect.AspectFit,
            },
        },
        new ContentPage {
            Title = "Fill",
            Content = new Image {
                Source = ImageSource.FromResource("xamarin"),
                Aspect = Aspect.Fill,
            },
        },
    },
};
```

The three Aspect values and their respective meaning are:

- AspectFill to preserve the aspect ratio and to scale the image to fill the available space completely, possibly cropping parts of the image,

- AspectFit to preserve the aspect ratio and to scale the image to fill at least one dimension of the available space, possibly leaving some blank space next to the image, and

- Fill to fill the available space without preserving the aspect ratio.

Figure 7.2: Page with one centered image, either with `Aspect` property set to `AspectFill` (left), `AspectFit` (center) or `Fill` (right).

7.3 Panning and zooming images using a web view

There might be a situation where you want to display an image with pan and zoom functionality. Although you can implement custom renderers with gesture handling, as described in Section 3.2 about gesture-based interaction, there is a much simpler alternative using a `WebView`. It is a visual element displaying arbitrary HTML.

Adding a `WebView` to our `MainPage` is simple. The most important property is the `Source`, which is set to a new `HtmlWebViewSource`.

```
MainPage = new ContentPage {
    Padding = new Thickness(0, Device.OS == TargetPlatform.iOS ? 20 : 0,
        0, 0),
    Content = new WebView {
        Source = new HtmlWebViewSource {
            Html = "<html><body><img src=\"xamarin.png\"/></body></html>",
            BaseUrl = BaseUrl,
        },
    },
};
```

The HTML code contains an image referring to an image file "xamarin.png". In order to let the WebView search for the file in the correct directory, we need to specify the BaseUrl, which is different depending on the device platform. Therefore, we define a public static property of our App class.

```
public static string BaseUrl;
```

It is initialized within the platform-specific code:

- On Android – within OnCreate – we set BaseUrl to a constant value.

```
App.BaseUrl = "file:///android_asset/";
```

- On iOS – within FinishedLaunching – we initialize the BaseUrl with the main bundle path.

```
App.BaseUrl = NSBundle.MainBundle.BundlePath;
```

These few lines of code are already sufficient to show an image with panning and zooming. On Android, however, zooming is not yet enabled. We need to add a custom renderer for the WebView element. To do so, we create a new empty class called "ZoomableWebViewRenderer" within the Android project and add an assembly attribute right after the using statements:

```
[assembly:ExportRenderer(typeof(WebView), typeof(ZoomableWebViewRenderer))]
```

The ZoomableWebViewRenderer is derived from the default WebViewRenderer. It only adjusts two settings related to the zoom controls. It is important to do that within OnElementPropertyChanged (and not within the constructor) and to do a null-check beforehand.

```
public class ZoomableWebViewRenderer: WebViewRenderer
{
    protected override void OnElementPropertyChanged(object sender,
        PropertyChangedEventArgs e)
    {
        if (Control != null) {
            Control.Settings.BuiltInZoomControls = true;
            Control.Settings.DisplayZoomControls = false;
        }
        base.OnElementPropertyChanged(sender, e);
    }
}
```

Now Android uses built-in zoom controls, but does not display additional buttons.

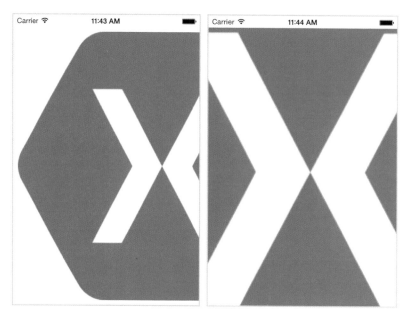

Figure 7.3: A WebView with an embedded image when starting the app (left) and after zooming and panning (right).

CHAPTER 8

Icons – More than small images

Some images, like the app icon, the launch image and toolbar icons, are treated a little differently than normal images. There are even differences between Android and iOS. Therefore we dedicate a whole chapter to those small icons.

8.1 The app icon

A prominent app icon is an important feature. Despite of its small size, there are extensive style guides for all platforms. Since app design is out of scope of this guide, we only focus on adding an existing icon to a Xamarin.Forms app.

iOS

On iOS we first need to convert the icon into different resolutions. The following Bash script converts the original image "xamarin.png" into several "icon*.png" images.

```bash
#!/bin/bash

for width in 57 114 120 72 144 76 152 29 58 50 100 40 80
do
    size=${width}x${width}
```

```
    convert xamarin.png -resize $size\> -background transparent -gravity
        center -extent $size icon$size.png
done
```

These images are then set as app icons, spotlight and settings icons: We open the iOS project options go to Build → iOS Application → Universal Icons and load the icons.

Android

On Android we first add the icon file to the "Resources/drawable" folder. Then we set it as the new app icon: We open the Android project options, go to Build → Android Application → Application icon and use the drop down menu.

Figure 8.1: The app icon on an iOS device.

8.2   Launch images for a splash screen

Current style guides don't recommend displaying a splash screen on app start, but encourage to speed up the app start as much as possible. Nonetheless, you might want to show a so-called launch image while certain preparation needs to be performed in the background. On iOS it is rather trivial to do so. On Android we will need to use some kind of workaround, since launch images are usually not supported.

iOS

On iOS the procedure is similar to the app icon. We prepare the launch image in three different sizes, possibly using the following script.

```bash
#!/bin/bash

for size in 320x480 640x960 640x1136
do
    convert xamarin.png -resize $size\> -background black -gravity center
        -extent $size launch$size.png
done
```

Then we set them as launch images within the iOS project options → Build → iOS Application → Universal Launch Images.

Android

On Android we need to display an image before LoadApplication is called. One possibility is to add a new "LaunchActivity" to the Android project:

```
[Activity(
    Label = "Icons",
    ConfigurationChanges = ConfigChanges.ScreenSize |
        ConfigChanges.Orientation,
    MainLauncher = true,
    Theme = "@android:style/Theme.NoTitleBar")]
public class LaunchActivity : Activity
{
    protected override void OnCreate(Bundle savedInstanceState)
    {
        base.OnCreate(savedInstanceState);

        SetContentView(Resource.Layout.Main);
    }

    protected override async void OnResume()
    {
        base.OnResume();

        await Task.Run(() => Thread.Sleep(10));
        StartActivity(typeof(MainActivity));
    }
```

```
}
```

Note the MainLauncher attribute: It causes the LaunchActivity to be the first activity when starting the app. (Make sure to remove this attribute in "MainActivity.cs".) The activity simply displays a layout stored in "Resources/layout/Main.axml", referring to the "android.png" image stored in "Resources/drawable":

```xml
<?xml version="1.0" encoding="utf-8"?>
<LinearLayout xmlns:android="http://schemas.android.com/apk/res/android"
    android:orientation="vertical"
    android:layout_width="fill_parent"
    android:layout_height="fill_parent">
    <ImageView
        android:id="@+id/launchImage"
        android:layout_width="fill_parent"
        android:layout_height="fill_parent"
        android:src="@drawable/xamarin"
        android:scaleType="centerInside" />
</LinearLayout>
```

As soon as the activity becomes visible to the user, it triggers the MainActivity to be started. The tiny delay of something like 10 milliseconds makes sure that the launch image is actually drawn before continuing with the next activity. The image will remain visible until the MainActivity is loaded, which is usually much longer than 10 milliseconds.

Figure 8.2: The launch image, as it is shown for a moment when starting the app.

8.3   Toolbar icons

Another common application for icons are toolbar items. As a small example we create an empty `label`

```
var label = new Label {
    Text = "",
    HorizontalOptions = LayoutOptions.CenterAndExpand,
    VerticalOptions = LayoutOptions.CenterAndExpand,
};
```

and add it to the `MainPage`:

```
MainPage = new NavigationPage(new ContentPage { Content = label });
```

Now we add two toolbar items. The first one has an `Icon` and will write "Xamarin!" on the `label`. Note that a toolbar icon refers to platform-specific local images, requiring us to specify filenames.

```
MainPage.ToolbarItems.Add(new ToolbarItem {
    Icon = Device.OS == TargetPlatform.iOS ? "Icon-Small.png" :
        "xamarin.png",
    Command = new Command(() => label.Text = "Xamarin!"),
});
```

On iOS we need to have a correctly sized icon available. Since we already added the Xamarin logo as an app icon, the 29-pixel version and the 58-pixel versions are located in the "Resources" folder named "Icon-Small.png" and "Icon-Small@2x.png". The latter with the "2@x" suffix is automatically used for retina displays. For different icons you need to prepare such images yourself and add them to the "Resources" folder with the same naming scheme "your_icon.png" and "your_icon@2x.png".

Another thing to consider is that iOS allows unicolored toolbar icons only. More specifically, there must be one color on a transparent background, while all colored pixels will be rendered blue. In our example there is a blue hexagon with a white "X" on a transparent background. Both, the hexagon and the "X" are rendered blue. Only the transparent background vanishes. Thus, when creating an icon set for an app, we need to consider these limitations.

On Android, the icon is automatically scaled and displayed with all its colors. For this reason – and the different design guides – it is essential to create separate icon sets for each platform.

The second toolbar item is plain text and, consequently, straight forward. Instead of specifying the `Icon`, we define a `Text`. When clicked, the `label` will display the string "Forms!".

```
MainPage.ToolbarItems.Add(new ToolbarItem {
```

```
    Text = "Forms",
    Command = new Command(() => label.Text = "Forms!"),
});
```

Figure 8.3: The navigation page with two toolbar items after clicking the Xamarin icon (left) and the "Forms" item (right).

CHAPTER 9

Fonts and vector graphics – Perfect quality on all screens

When working with raster graphics, you need to consider screens with different resolution. An alternative is to use scalable vector graphics. Although vector image formats like SVG are neither supported on Android nor iOS, we will propose a workaround using custom fonts. But first, let's see how to switch fonts in general.

9.1 Using custom fonts

High-quality apps with appealing design often require to use custom fonts for UI elements. A common file format is the True Type Font (TTF), which you will find on major font providers like dafont.com[1]. Fortunately, there is a way to include TTFs in a Xamarin.Forms app, although there are differences between iOS and Android.

Including custom fonts on iOS

On iOS you only need to add the font to the project file structure, register the font and you can use it within the shared code:

1. Add the TTF file to the Resources folder of your iOS project.

2. Edit the file properties:

---

[1]http://www.dafont.com/

- "Copy to output directory": "Always copy"
- "Build action": "Bundle resource"

3. Register the new font:

- Open "Info.plist" and click "Source".
- Add a new line via "Add new entry" and select "Fonts provided by application".
- Set the value to the TTF filename, in this example "smartphone.ttf".

Before looking into how to use the font within the shared code, we'll discuss how to add a custom font on Android.

Including custom fonts on Android

Adding a font to an Android project is slightly easier, but using it requires some native code within a custom renderer.

1. Add the TTF file to the Assets folder of your Android project.

2. Edit the file properties:

- "Build action": "AndroidAsset"

3. Write custom renderer for the visual elements that should use the new font.

The architecture of the custom renderer depends on the actual application. If you introduce a new default font for the whole UI, you might simply replace the renderer for the Label class. If you want to be able to switch between different fonts, you might want to derive a new label with a dedicated renderer.

In this example we will register a new FontLabelRenderer for the default Label using the FontFamily property, allowing us to define the font within the shared code. Consequently, the assembly attribute is as follows:

```
[assembly:ExportRenderer(typeof(Label), typeof(FontLabelRenderer))]
```

The renderer itself contains only one instruction: The Typeface of the underlying Control is loaded from the application Assets according to the filename written in the Element's FontFamily property.

```
public class FontLabelRenderer: LabelRenderer
{
    protected override void
        OnElementChanged(ElementChangedEventArgs<Label> e)
    {
```

```
        base.OnElementChanged(e);

        Control.Typeface = Typeface.CreateFromAsset(Forms.Context.Assets,
            Element.FontFamily);
    }
}
```

It is important to do the assignment within OnElementChanged and *not* in the constructor, because there the Element is not accessible, yet. Furthermore, if the elements changes frequently, you might want to add additional checks to avoid creating a new typeface each time. Otherwise the method CreateFromAsset will affect the performance of your app negatively.

Using custom fonts within shared code

Now we can use the new font within the shared code. The constuctor of our App class might look as follows:

```
MainPage = new ContentPage {
    Content = new Label {
        Text = "[smartphone]",
        FontFamily = Device.OS == TargetPlatform.iOS ? "[smartphone]" :
            "smartphone.ttf",
        FontSize = 54,
        HorizontalOptions = LayoutOptions.CenterAndExpand,
        VerticalOptions = LayoutOptions.CenterAndExpand,
    },
};
```

Again, we place a single centered label on the MainPage. For iOS, we can assign the name of our new font to the Label property FontFamily, which is "[smartphone]" in this example. For Android, however, we need the filename for the custom renderer. Therefore, we distinguish between the two operating systems via Device.OS.

The screenshot of the final example might unveil the reason for the strange brackets within the Text: These two symbols are rendered as two charging plugs!

9.2 Scalable vector graphics via custom icon fonts

Custom fonts allow us to illustrate our UI with icons. In contrast to using bitmaps, there are several advantages:

Figure 9.1: A label with a custom font. The charging plugs are generated with two extra characters.

○ Assuming you have a suitable icon font at hand, adding the icons to the solution is fast and easy. You only need to add and maintain a single file per platform.

○ Loading page with many icons will take noticeably longer than loading labels. The different font does not cost any time – except when loading the font once at app start. Furthermore, we won't see any delay between displaying the other visual elements and then the icons.

○ Icon fonts are – like vector graphics in general – scalable. Thus we don't need to prepare different resolutions, but will see optimal quality on any screen.

There are, however, some disadvantages as well:

○ Each icon can only consist of one color on a transparent background. We will be able to adjust the color via the font color and set a background color as well, but multi-color icons can't be converted to fonts.

○ Creating a font with custom icons requires a bit more time and special software (which is freely available).

In the following sections we will discuss how to find free icon fonts, how to create your own from a collection of vector graphics and how to work with icon fonts in a Xamarin.Forms solution.

Getting icon fonts

On the afore-mentioned website dafont you not only find fonts for normal text, but icon fonts as well, called "dingbats". For icons, there are dedicated sites like flaticon.com[2], that allow you to create your on collection of free icons and download them in various formats including TTF fonts.

Creating your own icon font

In case you don't find a suitable icon on a website offering TTF downloads, or if you get single vector images for your app from a designer, you might wish to create a custom icon font. The following steps describe the procedure using the free font editor FontForge.

1. (Optional, in case SVG graphics are not already available) You need to convert the images into scalable vector graphics (SVG): Open the images with the free vector image editor Inkscape and save them as "Plain SVG" files.

2. Scale the SVG images to a size of 1024×1024 pixels.

   You can use the bash command

   ```
   rsvg-convert original.svg -w 1024 -h 1024 -f svg -o scaled.svg
   ```

   or wrap it with a for-loop:

   ```
   for file in *.svg
   do
           rsvg-convert "$file" -w 1024 -h 1024 -f svg -o
               "${file/.svg/_scaled.svg}"
   done
   ```

3. Open FontForge and tweak two important settings:

   - Set a font name:
     "Element" → "Font Info"… → "Font name"
   - Set the glyph size to 1024 pixels:
     "Element" → "Font Info…" → "General" → "Em Size": "1024"

4. Double-click on a glyph to fill it with an SVG image.

5. Import the SVG.

---

[2]http://www.flaticon.com/

6. (Optional, in case you don't see the graphic)

   Display filled areas:

   "View" → "Show" → "Fill"

7. (Optional, in case the filled area is incorrect)

   You might need to fix the orientation of the contours, until the correct areas are filled:

   Double-click on a contour and click "Element" → "Reverse Orientation"

8. Export the font as a True Type Font (TTF) file:

   "File" → "Generate Fonts"

   (There might occur conflicts, which are usually not critical and can be ignored.)

Whether we downloaded an existing TTF file from the web or created our own icon font – we'll be able to include it in a Xamarin.Forms solution like a normal font. Since the fonts will display arbitrary icons as a translation of normal ASCII characters, we'll suggest a dedicated class with an easily readable translation table in the next section.

Working with icon fonts

To demonstrate the usage of icon fonts, we create a simple `MainPage` containing a `StackLayout` filled with three `StackRows`. Each row contains an icon and a label and is – to avoid duplicate code – defined in a separate class.

```
MainPage = new ContentPage {
    Content = new StackLayout {
        HorizontalOptions = LayoutOptions.CenterAndExpand,
        VerticalOptions = LayoutOptions.CenterAndExpand,
        Children = {
            new StackRow(VectorIcon.Like, "Like"),
            new StackRow(VectorIcon.Dislike, "Dislike"),
            new StackRow(VectorIcon.Settings, "Settings"),
        },
    },
};
```

A `StackRow` itself is a `StackLayout` with horizontal orientation, i.e. its child elements are arranged horizontally. The first child is a `Label` displaying the `icon` character with our `Icons` font and a rather large font size. The second child is a normal `Label`.

```
public class StackRow: StackLayout
{
```

```csharp
public StackRow(char icon, string text)
{
    Orientation = StackOrientation.Horizontal;
    Children.Add(new Label {
        Text = icon.ToString(),
        FontFamily = Device.OS == TargetPlatform.iOS ? "Icons" :
            "Icons.ttf",
        FontSize = 48,
        VerticalTextAlignment = TextAlignment.Center,
    });
    Children.Add(new Label {
        Text = text,
        VerticalTextAlignment = TextAlignment.Center,
    });
}
}
```

The VectorIcon is the important class in this example. It lists the corresponding character for each icon stored in the icon font. This allows an easy access at implementation time, even with code completion, like in the example code above: VectorIcon.Like.

```csharp
public static class VectorIcon
{
    public static readonly char Dislike = 'D';
    public static readonly char Like = 'L';
    public static readonly char Settings = 'S';
}
```

After adding the TTF file to the iOS project and registering it in the "Info.plist" – as described above –, we'll already see our new icons. On Android we not only need to add the TTF file to the Assets folder, but need to add a custom renderer to actually use the typeface for the underlying control:

```csharp
if (Element.FontFamily != null)
    Control.Typeface = Typeface.CreateFromAsset(Forms.Context.Assets,
        Element.FontFamily);
```

Automating the font generating process using a Python script

You can automate the process of creating the TTF file as well as the VectorIcon class. We propose the following python script, which collects all SVG files in the current directory and creates the TTF file using the FontForge scripting language as well as the VectorIcon.cs file.

Figure 9.2: Three labels illustrated with corresponding icons, which are generated from a custom icon font.

```python
#!/usr/bin/env python
from glob import glob
from os import system

glyphs = { hex(0x100 + i)[2:].rjust(4, '0'): svg[:-4] for i, svg in
    enumerate(glob("*.svg")) }

script = '''
    New();
    Reencode(\\"UnicodeFull\\");
    SetFontNames(\\"Icons\\", \\"Icons\\", \\"Icons\\");'''
for code, svg in sorted(glyphs.items()):
    script += '''
    Select(0u{0});
    Import(\\"{1}.svg\\");'''.format(code, svg)
script += '''
    Generate(\\"Icons.ttf\\");'''
system('fontforge -lang=ff -c "%s"' % script)

with open("VectorIcon.cs", 'w') as f:
    print >>f, "namespace VectorGraphics"
    print >>f, "{"
    print >>f, "    public static class VectorIcon"
    print >>f, "    {"
```

```
for code, svg in sorted(glyphs.items()):
    print >>f, "        public static readonly char {0} =
        '\u{1}';".format(svg, code)
print >>f, "    }"
print >>f, "}"
```

In our example with three icons, the generated FontForge script is as follows. After initializing a new font with name "Icons", it selects consecutive glyphs starting with unicode 0100 and assigns the corresponding SVG graphics:

```
New();
Reencode("UnicodeFull");
SetFontNames("Icons", "Icons", "Icons");
Select(0u0100);
Import("Dislike.svg");
Select(0u0101);
Import("Like.svg");
Select(0u0102);
Import("Settings.svg");
Generate("Icons.ttf");
```

The second part of the Python script writes the VectorIcon.cs file. It basically contains public static characters named after the SVG filenames and containing the respective unicodes from the FontForge script.

Remarks about icon buttons on Android

When using icons to represent buttons on Android, you might want to make the following adjustments:

- On Android Lollipop button texts will always be printed with uppercase letters. This impacts the resulting icon as well, if it is encoded with a lowercase letter. If you, for instance, have a "New document" symbol on letter "n", you might see the letter "N" or a completely different icon. To avoid this behavior, you need to set Control.SetAllCaps(false); within the font renderer.
- Buttons usually come with some padding and a minimum width. To obtain a really tight button, just as large as its icon, you need a few more lines within the renderer. To avoid the padding, set Control.SetPadding(0, 0, 0, 0);. And to avoid the minimum width, you need to set Control.SetMinWidth(0); *and* Control.SetMinimumWidth(0);. (Yes, you need both setters!)

CHAPTER 10

Web access – Accessing online resources

One of the most important features of modern mobile phones is the ability to access web content. After a short example on downloading information from a remote server, we will deal with a combination of sending and receiving data.

Web requests always cause a certain delay (at least 100 milliseconds, but usually much longer). Therefore, we take the opportunity to sneak into asynchronous background threading. This way the app will build the UI immediately and remain responsive to user interaction, while the content data is downloaded in the background.

10.1 Asynchronous web requests

To demonstrate asynchronous web requests with Xamarin.Forms we implement a web-based clock app. It will allow the user to ask a web server for the current time. While loading the JSON response, the UI will display a "Loading..." string and remain responsive to user input. For example, pressing the back button will allow the user to leave the page before finishing the download.

Of course, asking for the current time is just a very simple example and usually doesn't take very long. But still: The delay is noticeable and a responsive high-quality app should not perform such tasks on the UI thread. For more complex scenarios the importance of separating UI and background tasks is even larger.

We start with a MainPage containing a button that opens a new TimePage.

```csharp
MainPage = new NavigationPage(new ContentPage {
    Content = new Button {
        Text = "What time is it?",
        HorizontalOptions = LayoutOptions.CenterAndExpand,
        VerticalOptions = LayoutOptions.CenterAndExpand,
        Command = new Command(() => MainPage.Navigation.PushAsync(new
            TimePage())),
    },
});
```

The class TimePage is derived from ContentPage and is described in the following. It only contains a single visual element, namely a timeLabel centered on the page. Initially it shows the text "Loading...".

```csharp
readonly Label timeLabel = new Label {
    Text = "Loading...",
    HorizontalOptions = LayoutOptions.CenterAndExpand,
    VerticalOptions = LayoutOptions.CenterAndExpand,
};
```

The constructor of our TimePage only assigns the timeLabel to the page content.

```csharp
public TimePage()
{
    Content = timeLabel;
}
```

Now we deal with downloading the current time from the web. Therefore, we override the OnAppearing method of TimePage: It should request the time asynchronously and assign the result to the label text.

```csharp
protected override async void OnAppearing()
{
    base.OnAppearing();
    timeLabel.Text = await RequestTimeAsync();
}
```

Note that the execution of RequestTimeAsync is awaited using the await keyword. Because this is not allowed within the constructor, we chose to override the OnAppearing method. When overriding a method, you can decide whether to make it a synchronous or asynchronous method by adding the async keyword.

The RequestTimeAsync method will perform the actual web request. As indicated by the common suffix Async it is an asynchronous method. It creates a new HttpClient and requests a string from

```
{
    "time": "09:37:49 AM",
    "milliseconds_since_epoch": 1417685869463,
    "date": "12-04-2014"
}
```

The method JObject.Parse allows to convert the string into a json object, which can be used like a dictionary to access fields like "time". Note that you need to add the Json.NET packages for iOS and Android (listed as "Newtonsoft.Json" in the project's "Packages" folder).

```
static async Task<string> RequestTimeAsync()
{
    using (var client = new HttpClient()) {
        var jsonString = await
            client.GetStringAsync("http://date.jsontest.com/");
        var jsonObject = JObject.Parse(jsonString);
        return jsonObject["time"].Value<string>();
    }
}
```

Figure 10.1: An app for requesting the current time from an online resource. After pressing the button (left) we immediately see the next page (center). After a certain delay, the "Loading..." string is replaced by the current time (right).

10.2   Sending and receiving information

Besides receiving information from a remote server, a mobile app might need to *send* information as well. The following example will contain two buttons: one for sending a POST request to a test server[1] and one for receiving the transmission protocol. The server URL as well as the message to be transmitted are defined as constants:

```
const string url = "http://posttestserver.com/post.php";
const string message = "Xamarin.Forms!";
```

The server responses are written into two labels. We use a slightly smaller font size to fit everything on one screen.

```
var postResponse = new Label{ FontSize = 11 };
var getResponse = new Label{ FontSize = 11 };
```

The postButton will create a new StringContent with the previously defined message. Using a new HttpClient the content is sent to the server. Although POST is mainly for sending data, the server returns a response as well. We could use the status code for handling different errors. But here we simply write the response message to the postResponse label.

```
var postButton = new Button {
    Text = string.Format("Post \"{0}\"", message),
    Command = new Command(async o => {
        var content = new StringContent(message);
        using (var client = new HttpClient()) {
            var result = await client.PostAsync(url, content);
            postResponse.Text = await result.Content.ReadAsStringAsync();
        }
    }),
};
```

The getButton uses the previous response message to extract the URL of the transmission protocol. The exact format depends on the specific server. But usually POST requests are answered with a meaningful status code and possibly a URL, where the client can find the result of the respective operation. Finally, the result is written to the getResponse label.

```
var getButton = new Button {
    Text = "Get",
    Command = new Command(async o => {
```

---
[1]http://www.posttestserver.com/

```
        using (var client = new HttpClient())
            getResponse.Text = await
                client.GetStringAsync(postResponse.Text.Split()[8]);
    }),
};
```

Both labels and the two buttons are added to the MainPage using a StackLayout.

```
MainPage = new ContentPage {
    Padding = new Thickness(10, Device.OS == TargetPlatform.iOS ? 20 : 0,
        10, 0),
    Content = new StackLayout {
        Children = {
            postButton,
            postResponse,
            getButton,
            getResponse,
        },
    },
};
```

Note that this is a rather technical example app. Usually these POST and GET requests are performed asynchronously in the background and not visible to the user.

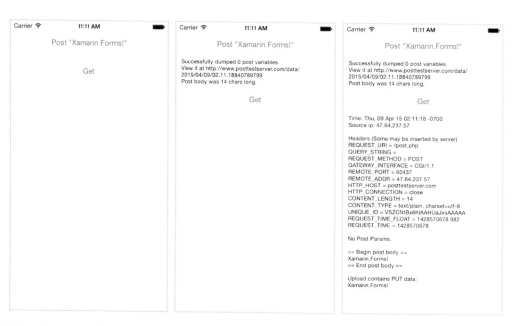

Figure 10.2: A demo app for posting a message to a test server (left). After pressing the "Post" button (center) and consecutively pressing the "Get" button (right) the server response is printed to the screen. As you can see from the "post body" at the bottom of the screen, the string "Xamarin.Forms!" was successfully sent to the test server.

CHAPTER 11

Geolocation – Navigating the real world

Determining the current GPS location of the mobile device is an important feature and used for many application scenarios. First, we will describe three approaches for determining the geolocation:

- Xamarin.Mobile (the easy but suboptimal approach to geolocation),
- Google Play Services (for better results on Android) and
- SimpleLocation (for better results with less code).

Hint: If you don't care for all these alternatives, try using SimpleLocation. This is, in our view, the way to do geolocation.

Furthermore, we will solve two related tasks:

- converting an address into coordinates – also known as geocoding – and
- displaying an interactive map.

11.1 Geolocation using Xamarin.Mobile

Xamarin.Mobile is a library for accessing common device functionalities like location, camera and contacts from shared code. It comes with an easy-to-use, platform-independent geolocation module. We don't recommend using it in production code, since it doesn't make use of the powerful location APIs of the Google Play services on Android. But in this chapter it will serve as a first reference solution, since getting the current GPS location is basically done in two to three lines of code.

We start by defining a public `Geolocator` object within the platform-independent `App` class.

```
public static Geolocator Geolocator;
```

Since the initialization method is slightly different for Android and iOS, we call it within the platform-specific code. In iOS' `FinishedLaunching` we call

```
App.Geolocator = new Geolocator { DesiredAccuracy = 50 };
```

and in Android's `OnCreate` we additionally need to pass the activity as context:

```
App.Geolocator = new Geolocator(this) { DesiredAccuracy = 50 };
```

Since iOS 8 we also need to add two items to the "Info.plist" file. We do so by either double-clicking the file from within Xamarin Studio and adding two strings within the "Source" view[1], or editing the file with a text editor of our choice and adding the following two entries right before the closing `dict` tag:

```
    ...
    <key>NSLocationAlwaysUsageDescription</key>
    <string>Can we use your location</string>
    <key>NSLocationWhenInUseUsageDescription</key>
    <string>We are using your location</string>
</dict>
</plist>
```

Within the `App` constructor we create a `MainPage` with one `Label`. The placeholder text indicates that the app is busy determining the location.

```
MainPage = new ContentPage {
    Content = new Label {
        Text = "Determining your location...",
        HorizontalOptions = LayoutOptions.CenterAndExpand,
        VerticalOptions = LayoutOptions.CenterAndExpand,
    },
};
```

Furthermore, we call a method `GetPosition`. This method is asynchronous and will continue running in a background thread after returning from the constructor.

---

[1]http://developer.xamarin.com/guides/cross-platform/xamarin-forms/working-with/maps/#3.1.ios

```
GetPosition();
```

The GetPosition method itself asks the static Geolocator for the current position. We pass a timeout of 10 seconds or 10000 milliseconds. For asynchronous method calls we can specify an action or function to continue with: Here we refer to the Task object t. We check its state and display either an error message or the obtained coordinates. The DisplayAlert method will open a pop-up window with the title "Location", the respective message text and an "Ok" button.

```
async void GetPosition()
{
    await Geolocator.GetPositionAsync(10000).ContinueWith(t => {
        if (t.IsFaulted || t.IsCanceled)
            MainPage.DisplayAlert("Location", "Couldn't determine
                location", "Ok");
        else
            MainPage.DisplayAlert("Location", string.Format("Latitude:
                {0}\nLongitude: {1}",
                t.Result.Latitude, t.Result.Longitude), "Ok");
    }, TaskScheduler.FromCurrentSynchronizationContext());
}
```

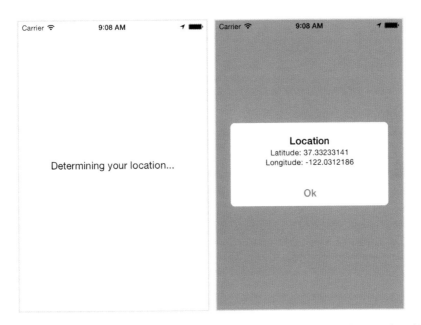

Figure 11.1: Locating the device. The determined coordinates are displayed within an alert dialog (right).

As indicated above, Xamarin.Mobile does not use Google Play services on Android. This has several disadvantages:

- ○ Xamarin.Mobile does *not* fuse different sources like GPS, Cell-ID and WiFi. Therefore, it lacks accuracy, speed and reliability.
- ○ When asking for the current location, Xamarin.Mobile needs to startup the GPS sensor and determine a new initial location. In contrast, Google Play services access the system-wide location, which might already be known from a previous request and – if there wasn't any major movement detected by the motion sensors – might still be sufficiently accurate. Thus, Google Play services are usually much faster.
- ○ Since Google Play services can combine different sensors, they can yield location requests with low required accuracy with less power consumption. Thus, Google Play services increase battery life.

11.2   Using Google Play services in favor of Xamarin.Mobile

To avoid the afore-mentioned disadvantages, we will create an example without Xamarin.Mobile. While an Android app benefits from increased accuracy, speed and battery life, the iOS performance will be almost identical and the source code is similarly short.

The shared project

Within the shared App class we define a locationLabel. Currently, its Text contains a placeholder string. After determining the location, it will show the GPS coordinates.

```
static readonly Label locationLabel = new Label {
    Text = "Determining your location...",
    VerticalOptions = LayoutOptions.CenterAndExpand,
    HorizontalOptions = LayoutOptions.CenterAndExpand,
};
```

The constructor of App initializes the MainPage with just that locationLabel.

```
MainPage = new ContentPage { Content = locationLabel };
```

Now we define two public static methods to enable the shared code to display either the determined location or an error string. The first one, DisplayLocation, takes two double arguments and assigns a formatted string to the label text.

```
public static void DisplayLocation(double latitude, double longitude)
{
    locationLabel.Text = string.Format("Latitude: {0}\nLongitude: {1}",
        latitude, longitude);
}
```

The second method is for displaying a plain error string:

```
public static void DisplayError(string message)
{
    locationLabel.Text = message;
}
```

The Android project

Before implementing a location-aware example app, we need to make a few preparations for the Android project:

- ○ Add the Xamarin.GooglePlayServices.Location from nuget.org to the Android project. (Dependencies like the Android support libraries and other Xamarin.GooglePlayServices packages will be added automatically.)
- ○ To avoid compiler errors on Android, you might need to set the target Android version to at least API 23 (Project Options → Build → Android Application → Target Android version) and the Java heap size to "1G" (Project Options → Android Build → Advanced → Java heap size).
- ○ Add the permission "AccessFineLocation" (Project Options → Build → Android Application → Required permissions).

Now we start to adjust the MainActivity. To be able to get connection callbacks and failures, we add and implement the two interfaces IConnectionCallbacks and IOnConnectionFailedListener:

```
public class MainActivity : FormsApplicationActivity,
                            GoogleApiClient.IConnectionCallbacks,
                            GoogleApiClient.IOnConnectionFailedListener
```

The first interface is implemented with the two methods OnConnected and OnConnectionSuspended. When successfully connected to the location services, we get the last device location and – if not null – ask the App to display the result.

```
public void OnConnected(Bundle connectionHint)
{
    var lastLocation =
        LocationServices.FusedLocationApi.GetLastLocation(googleApiClient);
    if (lastLocation != null)
        App.DisplayLocation(lastLocation.Latitude, lastLocation.Longitude);
```

```
}
```

When the connection gets suspended, we ask the App class to display an error. Here we could also display or even evaluate the cause. See the Google Play Services documentation[2] for more information on error handling.

```
public void OnConnectionSuspended(int cause)
{
    App.DisplayError("Couldn't determine position. Connection suspended.");
}
```

The second interface requires an implementation of OnConnectionFailed, which passes an error to the App as well. Again, we could make use of the argument result to get more information about the connection.

```
public void OnConnectionFailed(ConnectionResult result)
{
    App.DisplayError("Couldn't determine position. Connection failed.");
}
```

The OnConnected method above already uses the googleApiClient. It is defined as a member of Main-Activity

```
GoogleApiClient googleApiClient;
```

and initialized within OnCreate somewhere before loading the application.

```
googleApiClient = new GoogleApiClient.Builder(this)
    .AddConnectionCallbacks(this)
    .AddOnConnectionFailedListener(this)
    .AddApi(LocationServices.API)
    .Build();
```

Finally, we only need to connect the client when starting the activity

```
protected override void OnStart()
{
    base.OnStart();
    googleApiClient.Connect();
}
```

---

[2]https://developer.android.com/google/auth/api-client.html#HandlingFailures

and disconnect it when stopping the activity:

```
protected override void OnStop()
{
    googleApiClient.Disconnect();
    base.OnStop();
}
```

The iOS project

On iOS we first need a locationManager, which is a member of the AppDelegate.

```
readonly CLLocationManager locationManager = new CLLocationManager();
```

Within FinishedLaunching we need to ask for permission to access the device location – if the iOS version is greater or equal than 8.0.

```
if (UIDevice.CurrentDevice.CheckSystemVersion(8, 0))
    locationManager.RequestWhenInUseAuthorization();
```

Since iOS 8 we need to add the following two items to the "Info.plist" file again:

```
    ...
    <key>NSLocationAlwaysUsageDescription</key>
    <string>Can we use your location</string>
    <key>NSLocationWhenInUseUsageDescription</key>
    <string>We are using your location</string>
 </dict>
 </plist>
```

Afterwards, we add an event handler for any location updates. If the list of locations is not empty, we read the last entry and pass its coordinates to DisplayLocation in the shared project.

```
locationManager.LocationsUpdated += (s, e) => {
    if (e.Locations.Any()) {
        var coordinate = e.Locations.Last().Coordinate;
        App.DisplayLocation(coordinate.Latitude, coordinate.Longitude);
```

```
    } else
        App.DisplayError("Couldn't determine position");
};
```

Similarly to Android, we start the location updates when the app is activiated (i.e. the app gets into the foreground)

```
public override void OnActivated(UIApplication uiApplication)
{
    base.OnActivated(uiApplication);
    locationManager.StartUpdatingLocation();
}
```

and stop them when the app is resigned (i.e. the app is closed or moved to the background)

```
public override void OnResignActivation(UIApplication uiApplication)
{
    locationManager.StopUpdatingLocation();
    base.OnResignActivation(uiApplication);
}
```

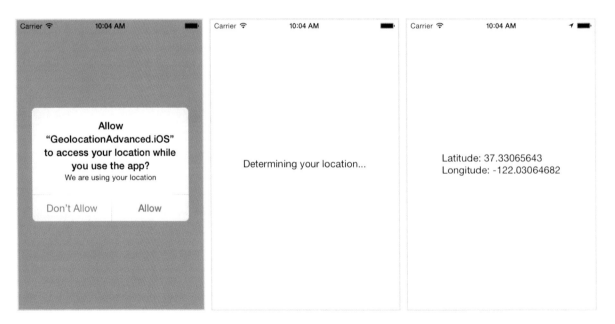

Figure 11.2: When starting the app for the first time on iOS, the user is asked for permission to access the location (left). After a short moment (center), the coordinates are displayed (right).

11.3 Using SimpleLocation for both simplicity and performance

As explained in the previous sections, we with to use Google Play Services for their superior performance. Unfortunately, the amount of platform-specific code is rather large. And providing a shared public static method called from Android and iOS code is not the clean, encapsulated code we're striving after.

Luckily, there is a NuGet package named SimpleLocation[3], which fulfills our needs: Under the hood it uses Google Play Services to exhaust Android's possibilities. At the same time, it keeps the interface for us very simple and lean. Let's look into an example with SimpleLocation.

The shared project

Our shared App gets a field locationManager

```
readonly SimpleLocationManager locationManager = new
    SimpleLocationManager();
```

Within the App constructor we simply create an empty, centered label

```
var label = new Label {
    VerticalOptions = LayoutOptions.CenterAndExpand,
    HorizontalOptions = LayoutOptions.CenterAndExpand,
};
```

and place it on the MainPage

```
MainPage = new ContentPage { Content = label };
```

Furthermore, we make the label display the current location as soon as the location is updated:

```
locationManager.LocationUpdated +=
    () => label.Text = string.Format("Latitude: {0}\nLongitude: {1}",
    locationManager.LastLocation.Latitude,
        locationManager.LastLocation.Longitude);
```

The LastLocation is formatted into a string and assigned to the label.Text.

---

[3]https://www.nuget.org/packages/SimpleLocation/

Finally, we start the location updates within the OnStart method of the App class. (Starting the location manager from the constructor might not work on iOS.)

```
locationManager.StartLocationUpdates(LocationAccuracy.Balanced, 1);
```

The two parameters are the required accuracy (Balanced in this example) and the smallest displacement (here 1 meter). You can further specify two intervals, which are only effective on Android.

The Android project

Within Android's MainActivity you need to pass a Context to the SimpleLocationManager. Simply place the following line above Forms.Init in the OnCreate method:

```
SimpleLocationManager.SetContext(this);
```

That's it. SimpleLocation will take care of the rest.

The iOS project

Again, we also need to add the following two items to the "Info.plist" file:

```
    ...
    <key>NSLocationAlwaysUsageDescription</key>
    <string>Can we use your location</string>
    <key>NSLocationWhenInUseUsageDescription</key>
    <string>We are using your location</string>
</dict>
</plist>
```

That's all you need to do on iOS. There is no platform-specific code required.

11.4   Geocoding

After getting GPS coordinates from the location sensors, we create a small example on how to convert a human-readable address into coordinates. This may come in handy when you ask the user for a location, but need coordinates for further processing.

Figure 11.3: Displaying latitude and longitude using SimpleLocation. The result is equivalent to the previous example.

To implement such a geocoding example, we use the Maps module of Xamarin.Forms. It is initialized at the very same place where Forms.Init is called, namely in OnCreate for Android

```
FormsMaps.Init(this, savedInstanceState);
```

and in FinishedLaunching for iOS:

```
FormsMaps.Init();
```

In the shared code, we define a searchBar. It is similar to an Entry element, but comes with buttons and events more dedicated to searching something. When pressing the "Search" button, we call an asynchronous method SearchAddress passing the search string and await the resulting coordinate representation. The latter are displayed as an alert dialog.

```
var searchBar = new SearchBar {
    Placeholder = "Enter an address",
    VerticalOptions = LayoutOptions.Start,
};
searchBar.SearchButtonPressed += async (sender, e) => {
    var coordinates = await SearchAddress(searchBar.Text);
    MainPage.DisplayAlert("Location", coordinates, "Ok");
```

```
};
```

Before implementing the SearchAddress method, we add the searchBar to the MainPage and make sure to have sufficient padding on the top edge of the iOS screen.

```
MainPage = new ContentPage {
    Padding = new Thickness(0, Device.OnPlatform(20, 0, 0), 0, 0),
    Content = searchBar,
};
```

The SearchAddress method is the place where the magic happens. We create a new Geocoder object and call an asynchronous method GetPositionsForAddressAsync. After awaiting a result of type IEnumerable, we convert it to a List and check whether it contains any element. If so, we return a string containing latitude and longitude of the first item. Otherwise, we return an error message.

```
static async Task<string> SearchAddress(string address)
{
    var geocoder = new Geocoder();
    var positions = (await
        geocoder.GetPositionsForAddressAsync(address)).ToList();
    if (positions.Any())
        return string.Format("Latitude: {0}\nLongitude: {1}",
            positions.First().Latitude,
            positions.First().Longitude);
    else
        return "No position found";
}
```

11.5 Maps

Another no less useful feature is to display a map, possibly with a set of pins identifying certain locations. With Xamarin.Forms' Maps module this can be easily done in shared code. We only have to initialize FormsMaps in OnCreate on Android

```
Xamarin.FormsMaps.Init(this, savedInstanceState);
```

and in FinishedLaunching on iOS:

```
Xamarin.FormsMaps.Init();
```

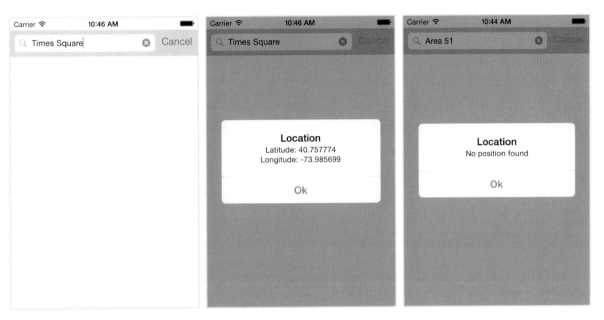

Figure 11.4: After entering a search string (left) the app displays the corresponding GPS coordinates (center). If the address isn't recognized as a valid geographic location, an error is displayed.

Then, in the constructor of our App class, we create an example map with one pin.

First, we define a new Position:

```
var position = new Position(52.516432, 13.377693);
```

This object is used to position a new Pin. The Label will be unveiled after clicking on the pin.

```
var pin = new Pin {
    Position = position,
    Label = "Brandenburg Gate",
};
```

Now we create the example map. Therefore, we need a mapSpan, which is the visible area. It can be defined with a position and a radius. Here we use the same position as for the pin and a radius of 250 meters.

```
var mapSpan = MapSpan.FromCenterAndRadius(position,
    Distance.FromMeters(250));
```

Using the mapSpan we create the map. Two additional properties set the map type to Street (i.e. no satellite imagery) and add the previously defined pin.

```
var map = new Map(mapSpan) {
    MapType = MapType.Street,
    Pins = { pin },
};
```

Finally, we add the map to our MainPage.

```
MainPage = new ContentPage { Content = map };
```

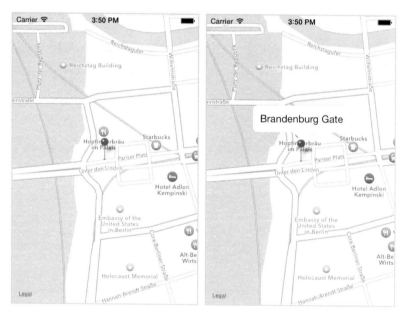

Figure 11.5: A simple map located at a specific location marked with a pin. A click unveils the descriptive label "Brandenburg Gate".

CHAPTER 12

Animations – Putting your app into motion

One of the core principles of Google's new "material design"[1] is: *Motion provides meaning.* Therefore, it is essential to use animation as a supportive technique to communicate the functionality of your mobile app. With Xamarin.Forms you can not only choose from a set of pre-defined animations, but can define your own as well.

12.1 Using pre-defined animations

Xamarin.Forms comes with a set of pre-defined animations like translation, rotation, scale and fading. In this example we will create a button that scales and rotates back and forth when pressed.

First we create a simple button

```
var button = new Button {
    Text = "Animate!",
    HorizontalOptions = LayoutOptions.CenterAndExpand,
    VerticalOptions = LayoutOptions.CenterAndExpand,
};
```

and add it to the MainPage:

---

[1]http://www.google.de/design/spec/material-design/introduction.html#introduction-principles

```
MainPage = new ContentPage { Content = button };
```

The button Command contains the actual animation code. Since we will await certain lines of code, the whole delegate has to be marked with the async keyword.

```
button.Command = new Command(async () => {
    button.ScaleTo(3, 1000, Easing.CubicInOut);
    await button.RotateTo(15, 1000, Easing.CubicInOut);
    button.ScaleTo(1, 1000, Easing.CubicInOut);
    await button.RotateTo(0, 1000, Easing.CubicInOut);
});
```

The first line scales the button to its triple size over a time of 1000 milliseconds. The easing CubicInOut lets the animation start slowly, than accelerate in the middle and decelerate when reaching the target state. Note that this line is not awaited. Thus the next animation is started immediately, without waiting for the first one to finish. The button is rotated to an angle of 15 degrees. This line is awaited: The execution of the Command pauses, until the rotation is complete. Because the time spans are equal, the scaling will just finish together with the rotation.) Last but not least, we repeat this combination of animations to scale and rotate back to the original state.

12.2   Defining custom animations

Xamarin.Forms' pre-defined animations allow you to translate, rotate, scale and fade visual elements. For any other needs, e.g. like color transitions, you can define custom animations.

Let's start with a button centered on the page.

```
var button = new Button {
    Text = "Animate!",
    HorizontalOptions = LayoutOptions.CenterAndExpand,
    VerticalOptions = LayoutOptions.CenterAndExpand,
};
```

Its Command contains a delegate which calls Animate, a method for starting a custom animation. We leave the optional name empty and define the animation to take half a second or 500 milliseconds to complete. The second and most important argument is a function depending on a variable x ranging from 0 to 1. The method body contains TextColor and Scale modifications given x: The color will be blue at the beginning and red after half a second, when x becomes 1. The scale grows from 1 to 3. You can also specify the step size with another optional argument.

Figure 12.1: Five frames of the animation. After scaling in and rotating to the right, the label is transformed back to its original size and orientation.

```
button.Command = new Command(() => button.Animate("", x => {
    button.TextColor = Color.FromRgb(x, 0, 1 - x);
    button.Scale = 1 + 2 * x;
}, length: 500));
```

Finally, we add the button to the Content of the MainPage.

```
MainPage = new ContentPage { Content = button };
```

12.3   Page transition animations

A minor, but noteworthy feature related to animations are animated page transitions. In fact, page transitions are animated by default. But you can disable them as well.

Let's create two buttons. The first one, button1, opens a new ContentPage with animation.

```
var button1 = new Button {
    Text = "Push with animation",
    Command = new Command(() => MainPage.Navigation.PushAsync(new
        ContentPage())),
};
```

The second one, button2, uses a second argument to PushAsync. Setting animated to false disables the page transition animation.

```
var button2 = new Button {
    Text = "Push without animation",
    Command = new Command(() => MainPage.Navigation.PushAsync(new
        ContentPage(), animated: false)),
};
```

Placing both buttons in a StackLayout on a ContentPage nested in a NavigationPage lets us experiment with both behaviors.

```
MainPage = new NavigationPage(new ContentPage {
    Content = new StackLayout {
        Children = {
            button1,
            button2,
```

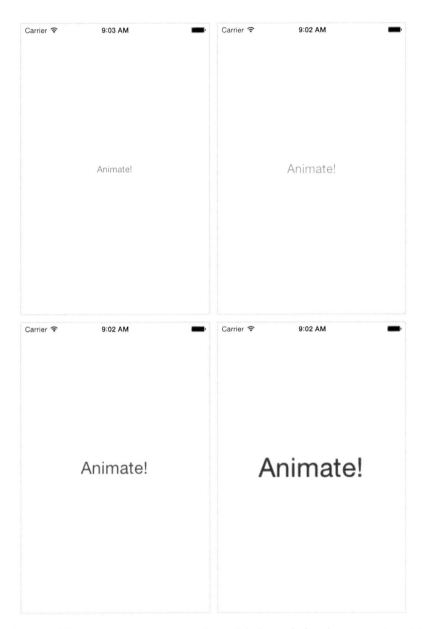

Figure 12.2: Four frames of the custom animation. While the label is scaled to three times its original size, the text color changes from blue to red.

```
        },
    },
});
```

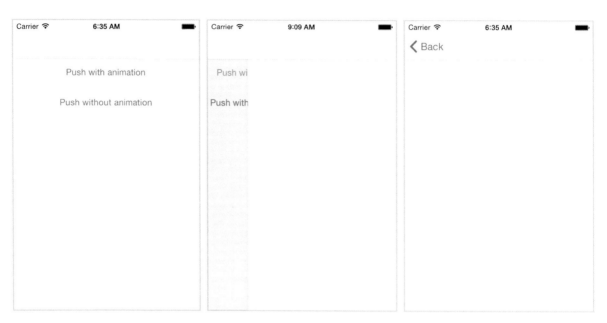

Figure 12.3: Opening a new page with or without animation. The screenshot in the middle shows a frame of the page transition, which is skipped when pressing the second button. In this example, the opened page is blank (right).

CHAPTER 13

Internationalization – Teaching your app new languages

In this chapter we want to prepare for the case your app is sold worldwide and you like to offer alternative languages.

Common approaches to this problem involve xml-based platform-dependent string resources. In contrast, we will demonstrate how to translate UI text using C# only.

We will propose two approaches with three major parts each:

1. Obtaining the current language code.

   This part is identically solved in both approaches using the cross-platform property `Culture-Info.CurrentCulture.TwoLetterISOLanguageName`.

2. Initializing the dictionary.

   The dictionary is either created at *compile time* or loaded at *runtime*.

3. Accessing vocabularies.

   The individual vocabularies are either made accessible as a *static class property* like `Translate.Hello-World` or as an *extension method* for strings like `"HelloWorld".Translate()`.

We will demonstrate a dictionary of static properties built at compile time as well as vocabularies loaded at runtime and made accessible with an extension method. But you can combine initialization and access differently if you wish.

13.1   Compiling a dictionary, accessible as static class properties

First we implement a static class Translate providing vocabulary properties for all UI strings and an initialization method allowing to initialize each string depending on the current system language. In case the languageCode parameter is not recognized, the Initialize method is called recursively with the default language English.

```csharp
public static class Translate
{
    public static string HelloWorld { get; private set; }

    public static string NowInThreeLanguages { get; private set; }

    public static void Initialize(string languageCode)
    {
        switch (languageCode) {
            case "en":
                HelloWorld = "Hello world!";
                NowInThreeLanguages = "Now in three languages!";
                break;
            case "de":
                HelloWorld = "Hallo Welt!";
                NowInThreeLanguages = "Jetzt in drei Sprachen!";
                break;
            case "fr":
                HelloWorld = "Bonjour le monde!";
                NowInThreeLanguages = "Maintenant en trois langues!";
                break;
            default:
                Initialize("en");
                break;
        }
    }
}
```

The initialization method is called at the beginning of the App() constructor. It uses the cross-platform property TwoLetterISOLanguageName, representing the current language setting of the executing device.

```csharp
Translate.Initialize(CultureInfo.CurrentCulture.TwoLetterISOLanguageName);
```

Now we can create a simple MainPage with a Label. Instead of initializing the Text property with a string like "Hello world!" we use Translate.HelloWorld.

```
MainPage = new ContentPage {
    Content = new Label {
        Text = Translate.HelloWorld + "\n" + Translate.NowInThreeLanguages,
        HorizontalTextAlignment = TextAlignment.Center,
        VerticalOptions = LayoutOptions.CenterAndExpand,
    },
};
```

Advantages of *extension methods* for vocabularies

- The reference to the Translate class is short and intuitive. It's like a command: *Translate "Hello world"!*

- Once all vocabulary is defined, you get automatic code completion, which is very handy for large dictionaries and long property names.

- You can easily refactor property names to reflect their content. If, for example, you changed the displayed text to "Hello, dear app user!", you can rename the corresponding property to HelloDearAppUser.

- Although the property definitions and initializations in the Translate class are rather lengthy, it is trivial code that can even be generated from other file formats like plain text or spreadsheets.

Advantage of creating the dictionary at *compile time*

- The translation is fast. Since the dictionary is built at compile time, displaying a translation is very cheap.

13.2   Loading a dictionary at runtime, accessible as extension method

Let us look into an alternative way to use multiple UI languages with Xamarin.Forms: The dictionary is loaded into memory at runtime. The vocabularies will be provided by an extension method.

We use a simple dictionary format stored plain text files. Each language file contains multiple lines, one for each vocabulary. The lines start with a key, separated from its translation by a colon.

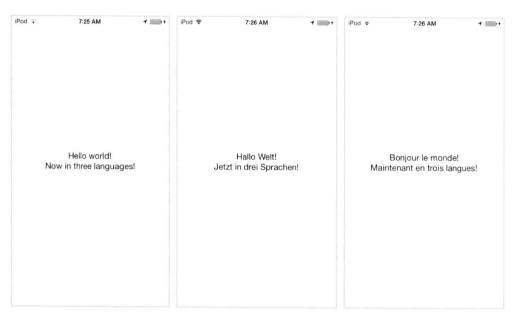

Figure 13.1: The app when started on devices with three different system language settings: English, German and French (from left to right).

Language file "dictionary_en.txt"

```
HelloWorld: Hello world!
NowInThreeLanguages: Now in three languages!
```

Language file "dictionary_de.txt"

```
HelloWorld: Hallo Welt!
NowInThreeLanguages: Jetzt in drei Sprachen!
```

Language file "dictionary_fr.txt"

```
HelloWorld: Bonjour le monde!
NowInThreeLanguages: Maintenant en trois langues!
```

The core functionality for this internationalization approach is implemented in a static Internationalization class. It contains a Dictionary with string keys and string values. In contrast to the previous approach, this dictionary will be loaded at runtime, thus we need to implement a LoadDictionary method, which will be called from the platform-specific code. The method reads a given file stream line by line and splits key and value at the unique separator ":". The Trim method removes remaining whitespace from the beginning and the end of both strings. Note that, if any key or value contains a colon, you might need to use a different separator. The Translate method is a simple dictionary lookup with a fallback return value in case the key is invalid. Using percent signs indicates a missing translation clearly visible on the UI. The this keyword in the argument list defines an extension method so that we can call it via dot notation.

```csharp
public static class Internationalization
{
    static Dictionary<string, string> dictionary;

    public static void LoadDictionary(Stream stream)
    {
        dictionary = new Dictionary<string, string>();
        using (var streamReader = new StreamReader(stream)) {
            while (!streamReader.EndOfStream) {
                var columns = streamReader.ReadLine().Split(':');
                dictionary.Add(columns[0].Trim(), columns[1].Trim());
            }
            streamReader.Close();
        }
    }

    public static string Translate(this string key)
    {
        return dictionary.ContainsKey(key) ? dictionary[key] : "%" + key +
            "%";
    }
}
```

As mentioned above, the LoadDictionary method is called from the iOS- and Android-specific code. On Android we can easily get the required file stream from Android assets. Therefore, we add the dictionary files to the "Asset" folder of the Android project, make sure to set build action to "AndroidAsset" and refer to them using the following lines of code during OnCreate:

```csharp
var language = CultureInfo.CurrentCulture.TwoLetterISOLanguageName;
var stream = Assets.Open("dictionary_" + language + ".txt");
Internationalization.LoadDictionary(stream);
```

On iOS we create an "Assets" folder by ourselves, add the dictionary files with build action "Content" and refer to them creating a new FileStream withing FinishedLaunching:

```
var language = CultureInfo.CurrentCulture.TwoLetterISOLanguageName;
var file = @"Assets/dictionary_" + language + ".txt";
var path = Path.Combine(Directory.GetCurrentDirectory(), file);
var stream = new FileStream(path, FileMode.Open, FileAccess.Read);
Internationalization.LoadDictionary(stream);
```

For easier file management you can also add the dictionary files to the shared project – since they are actually shared content – and link to them from both native projects.

Finally, on the MainPage we place the very same content as in the previous example, but using the new string extension method. The result is identical to the previous screenshots.

```
MainPage = new ContentPage {
    Content = new Label {
        Text = "HelloWorld".Translate() + "\n" +
            "NowInThreeLanguages".Translate(),
        HorizontalTextAlignment = TextAlignment.Center,
        VerticalOptions = LayoutOptions.CenterAndExpand,
    },
};
```

Discussion

In contrast to the previous approach, this solution has some major differences:

- It loads the dictionary at *runtime*. If done synchronously, this might slow down the app start a bit. But, alternatively, you could keep a dictionary in persistent memory and download an update from time to time. In contrast to the compiled dictionary, this gives you more flexibility to modify UI strings or to add additional languages after app release.

- The translation is implemented as an *extension method* for strings. This way you can write something like "HelloWorld".Translate().

- The dictionary is stored as a C# Dictionary<string, string>. Therefore – and because the dictionary is loaded only at runtime – you won't be able to use features like syntax completion or refactoring for the vocabulary. But it allows you to use more complex *keys* like "Now in three languages!".

The optimal implementation of UI internationalization depends on the particular application. For small apps it's usually sufficient to compile a dictionary. Larger apps, especially with more people like translators involved, you might want to retrieve it from external sources. Small dictionary files can easily be loaded at startup or asynchronously in the background. If it is possible to release a new app version after modifying the dictionary, we recommend to generate the `Translate` class from the previous section with an automated script from text files or a shared spreadsheet.

Remark on using keys instead of a reference language

Both proposed solutions define a dictionary based on a set of constructed, formal keys (with a representation close to English) and corresponding translations in a natural language like English, German or French. One could argue, we should use a reference language like English as keys. Although this might work in some cases, there are problems with terms that are equal in English, but require different translations in other languages. We would need to add a prefix or suffix indicating the required translation, e.g. "_noun" or "_verb". But then we already left the domain of a natural language and started to create a formal language anyway, which is why we suggest to use "international" keys and to treat English like any other language that requires translation.

CHAPTER 14

Timer – Never miss an action

For various reasons, you might want to delay an action or repeat it multiple times in a certain interval. While you can use built-in C# methods to do so, Xamarin.Forms comes with its own methods to start a timer. We will develop two apps for comparing both approaches.

14.1 Delaying an action

In this section, we will experiment with three approaches for delaying an action and discuss pros and cons. We will wrap each implementation into a button causing a flashing page background after a delay of one second, so that the strategies can be compared rather easily.

Thread.Sleep – synchronous

The most trivial approach is to pause the current thread for a certain period of time, 1000 milliseconds in this example.

```
new Button {
    Text = "Thread.Sleep",
    Command = new Command(() => {
        Thread.Sleep(1000);
        MainPage.Animate("", x => MainPage.BackgroundColor =
            Color.FromRgb(x, x, x));
```

```
    }),
},
```

Usually, especially when triggered by a UI element like a button, the current thread is the UI thread. Consequently, the UI will freeze for one second and won't respond to any other touch gestures. A better idea is to pause an asynchronous thread.

Thread.Sleep – asynchronous

We slightly modify the previous approach: Instead of pausing the current UI thread, we start an asynchronous task with Task.Run, which can be awaited.

```
new Button {
    Text = "Task.Run + Thread.Sleep",
    Command = new Command(async () => {
        await Task.Run(() => Thread.Sleep(1000));
        MainPage.Animate("", x => MainPage.BackgroundColor =
            Color.FromRgb(x, x, x));
    }),
},
```

This means that the app starts the execution, namely the one-second delay, and returns to the UI thread until the task is finished. Until then the UI remains responsive. Only after one second the app continues to execute the Command animating the page background.

Note that you might need to check whether the UI elements you want to access are still present after the delay. Since the app keeps responding to user interaction, the user might have left the current page or pressed another button.

Xamarin.Forms StartTimer

A third approach we want to discuss here is based on Xamarin.Forms' Device class. It is designed for repeating actions – as described in the following section –, but can be used for single actions as well. The StartTimer method requires two arguments: a TimeSpan and a function returning whether to continue repeating the timer. By always returning false, our function performs the desired background animation only once.

```
new Button {
    Text = "Device.StartTimer",
    Command = new Command(() => Device.StartTimer(
        TimeSpan.FromSeconds(1),
```

```
() => {
    MainPage.Animate("", x => MainPage.BackgroundColor =
        Color.FromRgb(x, x, x));
    return false;
})),
},
```

This solution is comparable with the previous one, since the UI thread is not blocked and the app remains responsive.

Figure 14.1: Three ways to delay an action. When pressing the first button, the UI freezes for a moment (center). After the delay of one second, all three buttons lead to a black page background (right).

14.2 Repeating an action

A slightly different problem is to repeat an action multiple times in a fixed interval. As indicated in the previous section, `Device.StartTimer` is capable of doing so.

To demonstrate the use of repeating actions, we create a "Count down" button.

```
var button = new Button {
    Text = "Count down",
    HorizontalOptions = LayoutOptions.CenterAndExpand,
    VerticalOptions = LayoutOptions.CenterAndExpand,
};
```

When pressing the button, it will count down from 3 to 0. First, we set the Text to "3". Then we start a timer with an interval of one second. In each iteration, it sets the current number by parsing the Button.Text and subtracting 1. While the number is larger than zero, the timer continues.

```
button.Command = new Command(o => {
    button.Text = "3";
    Device.StartTimer(TimeSpan.FromSeconds(1), () => {
        var number = float.Parse(button.Text) - 1;
        button.Text = number.ToString();
        return number > 0;
    });
});
```

Finally, we place the button on our MainPage.

```
MainPage = new ContentPage { Content = button };
```

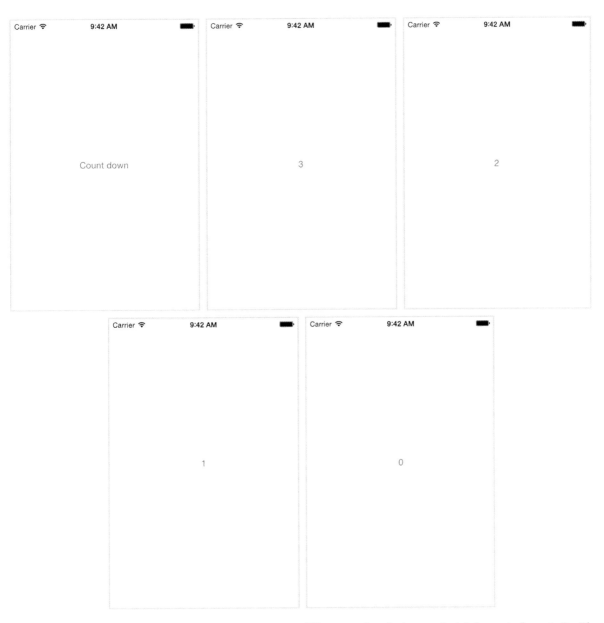

Figure 14.2: The initial screen and four consecutive states. When pressing the button, its label counts down to 0 with an interval of one second per state.

CHAPTER 15

Camera access – Taking pictures

A common but tricky task is to access the native camera tool from within Xamarin.Forms. There are libraries like Xamarin.Mobile or Xamarin.Forms.Labs which promise to support system features like contacts, photo albums and the camera. But apparently there are no up-to-date usage examples or – in case of Xamarin.Forms.Labs – no stable support for the current Xamarin.Forms version 1.3.

Therefore, this chapter will propose an implementation without additional dependencies to potentially unstable or outdated libraries. Besides a Xamarin.Forms integration with shared code we implement the actual system binding within the platform-specific projects for iOS and Android.

The shared project

First, let's look into the shared code. We will display an Image, which will be filled with content later. So we create a member:

```
readonly Image image = new Image();
```

Within the App constructor we create the page content, which is a simple button and the afore-mentioned image:

```
public App()
{
    MainPage = new ContentPage {
```

```
        Content = new StackLayout {
            VerticalOptions = LayoutOptions.Center,
            Children = {
                new Button {
                    Text = "Take a picture!",
                    Command = new Command(o => ShouldTakePicture()),
                },
                image,
            },
        },
    };
}
```

The button's click handler calls the event ShouldTakePicture. It is a public member and the platform-specific code parts will assign to it later on.

```
public event Action ShouldTakePicture = () => {};
```

Finally, we offer a public method for displaying the captured image:

```
public void ShowImage(string filepath)
{
    image.Source = ImageSource.FromFile(filepath);
}
```

The Android project

On Android we modify the MainActivity. First, we define a path for the captured image file:

```
static readonly File file = new
    File(Environment.GetExternalStoragePublicDirectory(
                        Environment.DirectoryPictures), "tmp.jpg");
```

At the end of OnCreate we can use the Xamarin's new Application.Current singleton pointing to our App instance and assign an anonymous event handler, which will start a new Intent for capturing an image:

```
(Xamarin.Forms.Application.Current as App).ShouldTakePicture += () => {
    var intent = new Intent(MediaStore.ActionImageCapture);
    intent.PutExtra(MediaStore.ExtraOutput, Uri.FromFile(file));
```

```
        StartActivityForResult(intent, 0);
};
```

Last but not least, our activity has to react on the resulting image. This is done by overriding the OnActivityResult method. The activity will simply push its file path to the shared ShowImage method:

```
(Xamarin.Forms.Application.Current as App).ShowImage(file.Path);
```

That's about it! Just don't forget to set the "Camera" and the "WriteExternalStorage" permission within "AndroidManifest.xml"!

The iOS project

For the iOS implementation we add the following code into FinishedLaunching after LoadApplication.

1. Create a new image picker controller referring to the camera:

```
var imagePicker = new UIImagePickerController { SourceType =
    UIImagePickerControllerSourceType.Camera };
```

2. Present the image picker controller, as soon as the ShouldTakePicture event is raised:

```
(Xamarin.Forms.Application.Current as App).ShouldTakePicture += () =>
    uiApplication.KeyWindow.RootViewController.PresentViewController(
    imagePicker, true, null);
```

3. After taking the picture, save it to the MyDocuments folder and call the shared ShowImage method:

```
imagePicker.FinishedPickingMedia += (sender, e) => {
    var filepath = Path.Combine(Environment.GetFolderPath(
                        Environment.SpecialFolder.MyDocuments), "tmp.png");
    var image = (UIImage)e.Info.ObjectForKey(new
        NSString("UIImagePickerControllerOriginalImage"));
    InvokeOnMainThread(() => {
        image.AsPNG().Save(filepath, false);
        (Xamarin.Forms.Application.Current as App).ShowImage(filepath);
```

```
    });
    uiApplication.KeyWindow.RootViewController.DismissViewController(true,
        null);
};
```

4. And finally, we need to handle a cancellation of the image taking process:

```
imagePicker.Canceled += (sender, e) =>
    uiApplication.KeyWindow.RootViewController.DismissViewController(true,
    null);
```

Note that this is a very minimalistic implementation. For real-world applications you should add various checks, like if there is a camera available or if the image was loaded successfully.

Figure 15.1: After pressing the button, the native camera app is started. The user takes a picture, confirms to use the photo and the image is displayed on the Xamarin.Forms page.

CHAPTER 16

Styles – Pretty up your UI

With version 1.3 Xamarin.Forms introduced a powerful concept for styling UI elements. Instead of assigning color, font size and similar properties to each single element or deriving UI elements with a certain style, in Xamarin.Forms we can instantiate a style itself and assign it to UI elements. Furthermore, there is the possibility to share styles across a page or even the whole application. And with implicit styles we can address all UI elements and define their default styling.

Throughout the following code examples we will introduce labels with different styling concepts. At the end of this chapter we will merge them into one MainPage and show the resulting screen.

Pre-defined styles: Quickly highlight titles and subtitles

The first and easiest way to make use of styles is to use a pre-defined style. The following titleLabel uses the TitleStyle and thus will be printed in bold letters.

```
var titleLabel = new Label {
    Text = "Title",
    Style = Device.Styles.TitleStyle,
};
```

All styles currently available in the Device.Styles class are:

- BodyStyle

- ○ CaptionStyle
- ○ ListItemDetailTextStyle
- ○ ListItemTextStyle
- ○ SubtitleStyle
- ○ TitleStyle

Custom styles: Define your own look

Alternatively, we can define a custom style as follows. We create a new Style for visual elements of type Label with one Setter. Setters are modifiers, each with the Property to be modified and its new Value. Our redStyle will have a red text color.

```
var redStyle = new Style(typeof(Label)) {
    Setters = {
        new Setter {
            Property = Label.TextColorProperty,
            Value = Color.Red,
        },
    },
};
```

Similarly to the titleLabel above, we create a new label and set its Style to our redStyle. So it will be displayed with red text.

```
var redLabel = new Label {
    Text = "Red",
    Style = redStyle,
};
```

Application resources: Share styles across the app

In a complex application you might want to define certain styles in one place and make them available to all classes working with the UI. Take the following greenStyle, for instance:

```
var greenStyle = new Style(typeof(Label)) {
    Setters = {
        new Setter {
            Property = Label.TextColorProperty,
            Value = Color.Green,
        },
```

```
    },
};
```

Let's assume we can't assign it to a label directly. We can, however, store it in the Xamarin.Forms application resources. They are always accessible through the static application field `Application.Current`. Note that we need to instantiate a new `ResourceDictionary` when writing to it the very first time.

```
Application.Current.Resources = new ResourceDictionary();
Application.Current.Resources.Add("green", greenStyle);
```

The key "green" can be arbitrarily chosen and is used for accessing the style later. For example, the following greenLabel applies the green style via the application resources and will be printed in green text color.

```
var greenLabel = new Label {
    Text = "Green",
    Style = Application.Current.Resources["green"] as Style,
};
```

Implicit styles: Address *all* UI elements

Finally, we look into implicit styles – a way to modify the styling of UI elements without explicitly assigning a style to each of them. First, we define a new style with blue text color.

```
var blueStyle = new Style(typeof(Label)) {
    Setters = {
        new Setter {
            Property = Label.TextColorProperty,
            Value = Color.Blue,
        },
    },
};
```

Now we add it to the application's Resources *without* specifying a key. This will indicate that this style is to be applied to *all* UI elements of the respective type Label.

```
Application.Current.Resources.Add(blueStyle);
```

Thus, the following `normalLabel` will be displayed with blue text color, although there is no style applied nor text color set.

```
var normalLabel = new Label {
    Text = "Normal",
};
```

Now let's put all labels together into one `MainPage` and look at the results.

```
MainPage = new ContentPage {
    Content = new StackLayout {
        VerticalOptions = LayoutOptions.CenterAndExpand,
        HorizontalOptions = LayoutOptions.CenterAndExpand,
        Children = {
            titleLabel,
            redLabel,
            greenLabel,
            normalLabel,
        },
    },
};
```

As you can see, the pre-defined title style, the explicitly assigned custom styles as well the implicit style for the last label are displayed correctly. In a real-life application with many pages and even more UI elements, Xamarin.Forms' styling concept is a powerful tool to separate the page layout from a corporate styling.

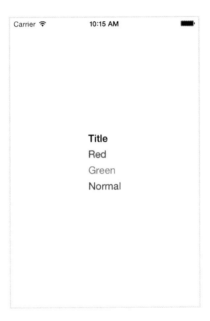

Figure 16.1: Four labels with different styles, either pre-defined or individually defined.

CHAPTER 17

Bindings – Linking UI and business logic

This chapter will deal with the interaction between UI elements and potential business logic. In order to react on UI events like a changed text of an entry field or a new slider position, we usually have to subscribe an event handler to the corresponding events. And in some cases it is important to unsubscribe afterwards in order to prevent the potentially long-living event handler from holding on to the UI element.

In the following sections, we will discuss three advanced concepts to link properties of one or multiple objects and to act or react in a certain way depending on other properties. While data binding has always been a feature of Xamarin.Forms, behaviors and triggers entered the stage in version 1.3.

17.1 Bindings

Let's start with bindings, a concept to link different properties like a slider position and a label text or the background color. To create a very simple binding example, we start with exactly those UI elements: a Slider with a default range from 0.0 to 1.0 as well as a Label with centered text alignment.

```
var slider = new Slider();
var label = new Label{ HorizontalTextAlignment = TextAlignment.Center };
```

We place them into a Stacklayout and add it to the content page.

```
MainPage = new ContentPage {
    Content = new StackLayout {
        VerticalOptions = LayoutOptions.Center,
        Children = {
            slider,
            label,
        },
    },
};
```

The label is meant to display the value of the slider. We could subscribe an event handler to the latter's ValueChanged event and set the text accordingly. Alternatively, we can bind the label text to the slider value. First, we need to set the label's BindingContext, i.e. the object which all bindings are referring to. And we set the binding of the label's TextProperty to the slider's ValueProperty. In this case, we might want to specify the stringFormat with two decimal places. (Otherwise the default format will contain up to 15 decimal places.)

```
label.BindingContext = slider;
label.SetBinding(Label.TextProperty, new
    Binding(Slider.ValueProperty.PropertyName, stringFormat: "{0:0.00}"));
```

You often see the second line like label.SetBinding(Label.TextProperty, new Binding("Value", ...)). We recommend using Slider.ValueProperty.PropertyName instead of "Value", because this way you can't have any typos within the string and both the compiler and the code completion help you to avoid mistakes. Furthermore – when creating your own bindable objects with bindable properties – you can easily refactor property names.

So, whenever we move the slider, the text is updated.

As a second, slightly more complex example, we want to bind the background color of the content page to the slider's position. Since the conversion between a floating point value and an RGB color is obviously nontrivial, we need to implement a converter.

```
public class DoubleToColorConverter: IValueConverter
{
    public object Convert(object value, Type targetType, object parameter,
        CultureInfo culture)
    {
        return Color.FromHsla((double)value, 0.7, 0.7);
    }

    public object ConvertBack(object value, Type targetType, object
        parameter, CultureInfo culture)
    {
```

```
        throw new NotImplementedException();
    }
}
```

It implements the IValueConverter interface with methods, Convert and ConvertBack. The Convert method takes a double value and creates a color from hue (the value), saturation (always 0.7) and luminosity (always 0.7). As long as our binding will only convert the slider position into a background color and not vice versa, we don't need to implement the second method.

Using this DoubleToColorConverter we can define the binding similarly to the one above. Instead of specifying a stringFormat, we pass an instance of the converter class.

```
MainPage.BindingContext = slider;
MainPage.SetBinding(VisualElement.BackgroundColorProperty, new
    Binding(Slider.ValueProperty.PropertyName, converter: new
    DoubleToColorConverter()));
```

So the slider not only controls the label text, but the background color as well. The screenshot below shows three example states.

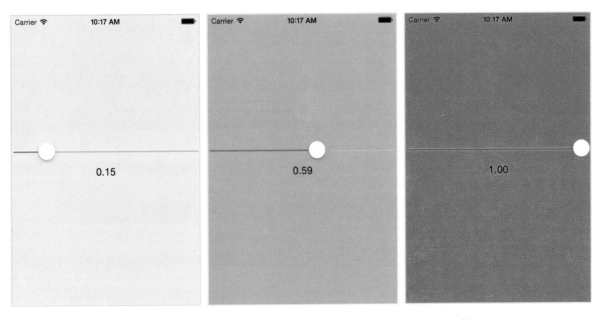

Figure 17.1: A slider controlling the label text below and the background color of the content page.

17.2   Behaviors

Sometimes a property is not only linked to another one, but the connection can be described as "behavior". For instance, an entry field might get an alarming background color if the entered text is invalid. By implementing the behavior independent of the specific UI element itself, we increase code reusability and readability.

Let's define a simple `Entry` centered on the `ContentPage`. It gets the behavior `LimitedLength`, which will check the length of the entered text and adjusts the text color accordingly. But at the moment, we don't have to know the details. We simply define it to behave like an entry with limited length.

```
MainPage = new ContentPage {
    Content = new Entry {
        VerticalOptions = LayoutOptions.CenterAndExpand,
        Behaviors = { new LimitedLength() },
    },
};
```

The `LimitedLength` behavior is implemented as follows. When attached to or detached from a view, it subscribes or unsubscribes an event handler `HandleTextChanged`. The handler itself sets the `TextColor` of the sender to `Default` or `Red` depending on the `Text.Length`.

```
public class LimitedLength : Behavior<Entry>
{
    protected override void OnAttachedTo(Entry bindable)
    {
        bindable.TextChanged += HandleTextChanged;
    }

    protected override void OnDetachingFrom(Entry bindable)
    {
        bindable.TextChanged -= HandleTextChanged;
    }

    static void HandleTextChanged(object sender, TextChangedEventArgs e)
    {
        var entry = sender as Entry;
        entry.TextColor = entry.Text.Length < 10 ? Color.Default :
            Color.Red;
    }
}
```

So when entering a long string, the text color remains black until the tenth character is entered. Then the input is highlighted with red color to indicate an invalid entry.

Figure 17.2: An entry element with default text color. After entering ten or more characters, a coupled length checker sets a red text color.

17.3 Triggers

A different approach to react on user input is to use triggers. Xamarin.Forms provides four types of triggers, which we will plug into one joint example application. The app will contain two entry fields and a label to display additional information. Both the nameEntry and the ageEntry have an empty Text and an informative Placeholder. (Although skipping the Text property would yield the same result, we need to set it to an empty string in order to get the triggers working properly.)

```
var nameEntry = new Entry {
    Text = "",
    Placeholder = "Name",
};
```

```
var ageEntry = new Entry {
    Text = "",
    Placeholder = "Age",
};
```

The infoLabel will have its text horizontally centered. Its HeightRequest is set to a fixed value in order to prevent the whole layout to jump up and down when the label text is filled or cleared.

```
var infoLabel = new Label {
    HorizontalTextAlignment = TextAlignment.Center,
    HeightRequest = 20,
};
```

We place all three elements centered on the page using a StackLayout. In the following we will add different types of triggers that will implement visual feedback depending on the user input.

```
MainPage = new ContentPage {
    Content = new StackLayout {
        VerticalOptions = LayoutOptions.CenterAndExpand,
        Children = {
            nameEntry,
            ageEntry,
            infoLabel,
        },
    },
};
```

Property triggers

The first type of triggers are property triggers. They observe a certain property and apply their setters as soon as a pre-defined value is reached.

In this example, we will set a blue background color, when the user enters the name "Robert". First, we implement the corresponding setter.

```
var blueBackground = new Setter {
    Property = VisualElement.BackgroundColorProperty,
    Value = Color.FromRgba(65, 149, 223, 127),
};
```

The trigger for visual elements of type Entry observes the TextProperty and – as soon as the Value is "Robert" – applies the blueBackground setter.

```
var textIsRobert = new Trigger(typeof(Entry)) {
    Property = Entry.TextProperty,
    Value = "Robert",
```

```
    Setters = { blueBackground },
};
```

Last but not least, we only need to add the trigger to the nameEntry.

```
nameEntry.Triggers.Add(textIsRobert);
```

Styles with property triggers

We can add triggers to styles as well. So we could define a triggerStyle containing the textIsRobert trigger

```
var triggerStyle = new Style(typeof(Entry)) {
    Triggers = { textIsRobert },
};
```

and attach the style to the nameEntry:

```
nameEntry.Style = triggerStyle;
```

Data triggers

Data triggers are similar to property triggers, but

- can observe a different UI element via bindings and
- can derive more complex data using value converters.

In this example we want the infoLabel to display an informational text as long as the text of the nameEntry is empty. So we define a sayEnterName setter

```
var sayEnterName = new Setter {
    Property = Label.TextProperty,
    Value = "Please enter a name.",
};
```

and add it to a noName trigger for UI elements of type Label:

```
var noName = new DataTrigger(typeof(Label)) {
    Binding = new Binding("Text.Length", source: nameEntry),
    Value = 0,
    Setters = { sayEnterName },
};
```

In this case we only evaluate the Length property of the entry text. Using a converter we could refer to deducted information like "valid" or "too long" as well. Our converter would simply need to convert a string input value into a bool return value.

Finally, we add the noName trigger to the infoLabel. Like a property trigger, the data trigger is assigned to the UI element it modifies, although it listens to a different input element.

```
infoLabel.Triggers.Add(noName);
```

Event triggers

Maybe the most natural type of triggers are event triggers. They listen to a certain event and react with a trigger action. Such an action might be the validation of a numerical input. Depending on whether the entered text can be converted to a floating-point number, the TextColor is set to either the default color or Red.

```
public class NumericValidationTriggerAction : TriggerAction<Entry>
{
    protected override void Invoke(Entry sender)
    {
        double result;
        var isValid = double.TryParse(sender.Text, out result);
        sender.TextColor = isValid ? Color.Default : Color.Red;
    }
}
```

With a new instance of our NumericValidationTriggerAction we can define a new EventTrigger observing the "TextChanged" event of the ageEntry. Whenever the text changes, the trigger action is invoked and the TextColor is updated accordingly.

```
ageEntry.Triggers.Add(new EventTrigger {
    Event = "TextChanged",
    Actions = { new NumericValidationTriggerAction() },
});
```

Multi triggers

The last type of triggers are multi triggers. They allow us to apply setters when multiple conditions are met. For this example, we want the infoLabel to display the greeting "Hi Peter!" when the entered name is "Peter" and the age is "30". Therefore, we define the sayHiPeter setter as follows.

```
var sayHiPeter = new Setter {
    Property = Label.TextProperty,
    Value = "Hi Peter!",
};
```

We use it to create a peter30 trigger with two conditions: The Text of the nameEntry has to have the Value "Peter". And the Text of the ageEntry has to have the Value "30". Since we refer to a different UI element than which will be modified by the setter, we need to use BindingConditions. Otherwise we could use PropertyConditions as well.

```
var peter30 = new MultiTrigger(typeof(Label)) {
    Conditions = {
        new BindingCondition {
            Binding = new Binding(Label.TextProperty.PropertyName, source:
                nameEntry),
            Value = "Peter",
        },
        new BindingCondition {
            Binding = new Binding(Label.TextProperty.PropertyName, source:
                ageEntry),
            Value = "30",
        },
    },
    Setters = { sayHiPeter },
};
```

Now we simply add the peter30 trigger to the infoLabel. Whenever both conditions are met, the sayHiPeter setting will change the Text property of this label.

```
infoLabel.Triggers.Add(peter30);
```

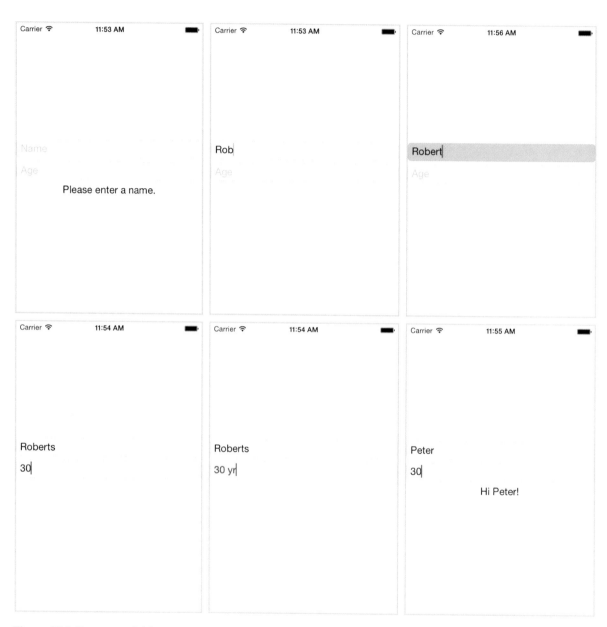

Figure 17.3: Two entry fields with various triggered UI responses: An empty name field causes the info label below to display a hint. The name "Robert" is highlighted with blue background color using a property trigger. The age is checked for numerical validity. And the combination of name "Peter" and age "30" will display a personal greeting.

CHAPTER 18

Cross-platform strategies – Combine native and shared code

This book focuses on building cross-platform apps with Xamarin.Forms. The main benefit of this framework is to write code once and compile it for iOS, Android and possibly Windows Phone. Although you can achieve quite a lot with shared code alone, we've seen examples where you need to implement some parts for each platform individually. We covered tiny modifications like an iOS-specific padding to preserve space for the status bar as well as more complex examples like gesture detection or accessing the camera.

This chapter will focus on such cross-platform code-sharing strategies and will compare six different approaches:

- `Device.OS` or `Device.OnPlatform`
- conditional compilation
- partial classes
- `DependencyService`
- custom renderers
- AppDelegate and MainActivity

Throughout the chapter we will build one minimalistic app displaying seven labels, each displaying a platform-specific text each of which is generated with a different strategy. All labels will be added to a vertical `StackLayout` centered on the `MainPage`:

```
var stack = new StackLayout {
    VerticalOptions = LayoutOptions.CenterAndExpand,
    HorizontalOptions = LayoutOptions.CenterAndExpand,
```

```
};
MainPage = new ContentPage { Content = stack };
```

Device.OS or Device.OnPlatform

Xamarin.Forms comes with a handy Device class containing two fields for distinguishing between different platforms. If you need tiny modifications like a different padding, a different font size or – as in our artificial case – a slightly different text, this is the first choice.

You can either access the current OS (operating system) and compare it to one of three TargetPlatforms

```
stack.Children.Add(new Label {
    Text = Device.OS == TargetPlatform.iOS ? "Hello iOS target!" : "Hello
        Android target!",
});
```

or call a method that returns one of three input values depending on the current platform:

```
stack.Children.Add(new Label {
    Text = Device.OnPlatform<string>("Hello iOS platform!", "Hello Android
        platform!", "Hello Windows platform!"),
});
```

The latter is specifically useful if you have different values for all three platforms.

Conditional compilation

To obtain minor differences depending on the executing operation system, you can use conditional compilation as well. In contrast to the previous approach, only one variant is *compiled*.

```
stack.Children.Add(new Label {
    #if __IOS__
    Text = "Hello __iOS__!",
    #elif __ANDROID__
    Text = "Hello __Android__!",
    #endif
});
```

The advantage is that, e.g., the Android part doesn't have to compile on iOS and vice versa. This might be useful if the signature of a method on Android differs from its iOS counterpart. On the other hand, when implementing, e.g., the iOS code, there won't be code checking, completion, syntax highlighting and refactoring support for the Android part. It's like commenting out one part of the code – with all its pitfalls.

Partial classes

We are approaching a series of more complex strategies. They are characterized by spreading code across shared and platform-specific projects. For tiny code adaptations they are probably not worth the effort. But when implementing more evolved classes and modules, you might want to create separate files anyway.

A first possibility to spread code across multiple files is using partial classes. We can define such a class in shared code and add parts of its implementation in the platform-specific projects. It is, however, important to place all parts into the same namespace, which is usually the shared one.

Shared code

Let's start with adding a new instance of a `PartialLabel`.

```
stack.Children.Add(new PartialLabel());
```

This `PartialLabel` is a custom partial class deriving from Xamarin.Forms' `Label`. Here, within the platform-independent code, we don't add any implementation.

```
public partial class PartialLabel: Label
{
}
```

iOS code

In the iOS project – but in the *same namespace* like the shared code – we add a public constructor. It simply sets the iOS-specific `Text`.

```
namespace CrossPlatform
{
    public partial class PartialLabel
    {
```

```
        public PartialLabel()
        {
            Text = "Hello iOS part!";
        }
    }
}
```

Android code

Similarly on Android, we implement the constructor with an Android-related Text.

```
namespace CrossPlatform
{
    public partial class PartialLabel
    {
        public PartialLabel()
        {
            Text = "Hello Android part!";
        }
    }
}
```

DependencyService

Xamarin.Forms offers another way to access native features from shared code. It involves a Dependency-Service for registering native implementations of shared interfaces. The overall infrastructure is comparable to using partial classes.

Shared code

To demonstrate this approach, we add a label with a Text loaded from the DependencyService. We ask for an implementation of an interface IGreeting and access the property Hello.

```
stack.Children.Add(new Label {
    Text = DependencyService.Get<IGreeting>().Hello,
});
```

The interface is defined as follows. It contains one read-only property Hello.

```
public interface IGreeting
{
    string Hello { get; }
}
```

iOS code

Within the iOS project we need to create an implementation of the interface IGreeting. We will call the class Greeting and register it with an assembly attribute outside of the namespace, right below the using statements.

```
[assembly:Dependency(typeof(Greeting))]
```

The Greeting class basically implements the Hello property, returning a iOS-specific string.

```
public class Greeting : IGreeting
{
    public string Hello { get { return "Hello iOS dependency!"; } }
}
```

Android code

The Android implementation is almost identical. The very same assembly attribute registers the dependency:

```
[assembly:Dependency(typeof(Greeting))]
```

And up to the specific string the Greeting implementation is the same as well.

```
public class Greeting : IGreeting
{
    public string Hello { get { return "Hello Android dependency!"; } }
}
```

Custom renderers

Another strategy that affects files in multiple projects is to implement custom renderers. We already used this concept for creating views with custom appearance and interactive behavior. Especially in the context of platform-specific artifacts related to visual elements, this is a common strategy. In this example it is rather cumbersome to create custom renderers only to change the label text. But it demonstrates the concept sufficiently well and simplifies the comparison to competing approaches.

Shared code

In shared code, we first add a new label to our stack. But, since we don't want to influence all other labels with a custom renderer, we use a new class CustomLabel.

```
stack.Children.Add(new CustomLabel());
```

The CustomLabel is derived from Label and has no other properties.

```
public class CustomLabel: Label
{
}
```

iOS code

The iOS renderer is registered using an assembly attribute placed right below the using statements. It links our CustomLabel class with the CustomLabelRenderer.

```
[assembly:ExportRenderer(typeof(CustomLabel), typeof(CustomLabelRenderer))]
```

The renderer derives from LabelRenderer and sets a platform-specific label Text. Here we set the Text property of the Control, which is the native view element of type UILabel. Alternatively, we could set the Element.Text, which modifies the shared Xamarin.Forms element and results in modifying the Control anyway. So this is the more direct approach:

```
public class CustomLabelRenderer: LabelRenderer
{
    protected override void
        OnElementChanged(ElementChangedEventArgs<Label> e)
    {
        base.OnElementChanged(e);
```

```
        Control.Text = "Hello iOS renderer!";
    }
}
```

Android code

On Android both the assembly attribute

```
[assembly:ExportRenderer(typeof(CustomLabel), typeof(CustomLabelRenderer))]
```

as well as the renderer implementation

```
public class CustomLabelRenderer: LabelRenderer
{
    protected override void
        OnElementChanged(ElementChangedEventArgs<Label> e)
    {
        base.OnElementChanged(e);

        Control.Text = "Hello Android renderer!";
    }
}
```

are identical – up to the assigned string.

AppDelegate and MainActivity

Last but not least, we look into another common place for platform-specific code: the AppDelegate and MainActivity classes. Not only is this the entry point for initializing Xamarin.Forms and instantiating the App class, but we already used the OnCreate and FinishedLaunching methods for executing platform-specific code.

Shared code

Within the shared project we could add a new label

```
stack.Children.Add(new Label {
```

```
    Text = Greeting,
});
```

with a Text property referring to a public static member variable Greeting.

```
public static string Greeting;
```

So far we won't see anything, because Greeting is null by default and so far we didn't initialized this field.

iOS code

We place the initialization of App.Greeting into the FinishedLaunching method of the iOS app.

```
App.Greeting = "Hello iOS app delegate!";
```

Since the static member is always available, we can place this line anywhere within FinishedLaunching, but no later than LoadApplication, which refers to the value of Greeting.

Android code

On Android, we assign App.Greeting anywhere within OnCreate, but – again – no later than LoadApplication.

```
App.Greeting = "Hello Android activity!";
```

This concludes our comparison of several strategies for sharing code across cross-platform apps. The following screenshot shows the result of all the example code. Each label contains a platform-specific text generated with one of the methods described above.

The following table compares these strategies under the following aspects:

- ○ Android context:

    Whether Android's Context is automatically available from where the native implementation lives. E.g., the MainActivity has a Context property. But there is none in the shared code, where we would use Xamarin.Forms' Device or conditional compilation.

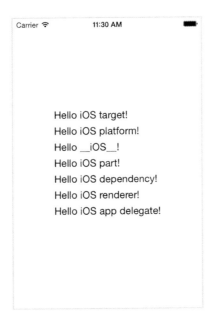

Figure 18.1: Seven labels with a platform-specific text, each generated with one of six different strategies.

○ Small overhead:

This criterion distinguishes between the "local" solutions like conditional compilation, that affect one file only, and the "global" solutions like custom renderers, that require classes in multiple projects.

○ Libraries available:

This is kind of a counterpart of "small overhead". If the native code is directly written in shared code, there are no native libraries available.

○ No cross-compilation:

Some approaches "cross-compile" the Android-specific code for iOS as well and vice versa. This is an issue if one part is not compilable on both platforms. But this only occurs when using the Device switch in shared code.

○ Code completion:

When using conditional compilation, you loose code completion, checking, syntax highlighting, analysis and refactoring support for the part that is currently deactivated.

Table 18.1: Comparison of the above-mentioned cross-platform code-sharing strategies. See text for a description of each criterion.

	Device	conditional compilation	partial classes	dependency service	custom renderer	MainActivity, AppDelegate
Android context					×	×
small overhead	×	×				
libraries available			×	×	×	×
no cross-compilation		×	×	×	×	×
code completion	×		×	×	×	×

A last request

Thank you for purchasing this copy of the Xamarin.Forms Kickstarter. If you found it useful for your daily work in cross-platform app development, I'd be glad to read your recension at Amazon. Such reviews make good books show up where they belong to: on the top.

Simply go to the Amazon website, search for "Xamarin.Forms Kickstarter", click on the book and then on "Write a customer review". Write a few words on what you liked (or didn't like) about this guide.

Thanks so much for your time. You're helping a lot.

Index

Made in the USA
Columbia, SC
31 January 2018